Harpoon

The Passion of Hunting the Magnificent Bluefin Tuna

By Capt. Corky Decker

Website: corkydecker.com
Contact: corkydecker@hotmail.com

Original art work on cover by artist Peter Graves
Contact: reddogllc603@gmail.com
Back cover photo from Megan Tibbets

ISBN-13: 978-0692956083 (Custom Universal)
ISBN-10: 0692956085

Printed in the United States of America

Library of Congress Control Number pending.

Billy Mac, this book is for you

Photo from McIntire Family

Authors Note

I have a very interesting view of the bluefin tuna fishery. I was around when Dana Kangas was storming NMFS in the 1970's fighting for a harpoon quota, and into the early 1980's with Jack Cadario and the Cobra putting out flag ends as fast as I could hand Jack another pole.

Then for thirty years I ran factory trawlers in the Bering Sea and tagged blue marlin in the South Pacific.

I returned back to the bluefin, the fish of my youth, the fish that shaped me and sent me down this path. I have never doubted that I would one day return to Maine, that was stamped on my soul at birth.

This book is finally going to print, three years in the making, I pray to the tuna god, that I did her proud on this one…

To all of you, too numerous to name who helped me get this work completed, you know who you are, a sincere thank you.

Captain Mark S. Decker 'Corky'

The Harpoon: Introduction written by Jefferson Morley

Book I Today

Book II Yesterday

BOOK III Tomorrow

Introduction:
The Harpoon

The harpoon was perhaps the very first tool of seafaring mankind. Thirty centuries ago, on the Peloponnesian peninsula in the eastern Mediterranean, the people honored Poseidon, the god of the ocean. He was a capricious deity of storms, calms, and squalls, a god to be appeased, respected and feared. In the ancient Greek imagination, Poseidon wielded a trident, a three-headed weapon used to spear fish, an early version of the what we now call a harpoon. Later in the same part of the world, the Romans honored Neptune as the god of the deep. Neptune carried a trident too, which he used to cause earthquakes, tidal waves and tsunamis. Several millennia later, in 1851, the American writer Herman Melville, who had worked on a whaling ship, wrote a novel that would become a classic. *Moby Dick, Or, The Whale* was, among other things, a story of men who harpooned giant fish for a living.

Why do mythic tales of the harpoon endure? Over millennia of human existence, the harpoon--like the fisherman's net and the baited hood--has never gone out of use, because it remains one of the most basic ways to catch fish. And fish are have always been staple of the human diet from ancient Greece to 21st century Tokyo, from the Mediterranean to Down East Maine.

The harpoon is the most intimate of tools. In *Moby Dick* the harpoon first appears first in the hands of Queequeg, the South Pacific sailor who toils slightly aloof from his white and Christian shipmates. Ishmael, the narrator of the book, finds himself drawn to Queequeg's simple integrity and unusual ways. The two men are randomly bunkered in the same room and come to enjoy an easy rapport. Ishmael admires his original style of grooming.

"He then donned his waistcoat and taking up a piece of hard soap on the washstand center table, dipped it in water and commenced blathering his face," said Ishmael. "I was watching to see where he kept his razor, when low and behold, he takes the harpoon from the bed corner, slips out the long wooden stock, unsheathes the head, whets it a little on his boot, and striding up to the bit of mirror against the wall, begins a vigorous scraping, or rather harpooning of his cheeks."

Ishmael learns that Queequeg comes from a royal family on his South Pacific island and will eventually have to return to claim his kingdom. In the meantime, "he proposed to sail about, and sow his wild oats in all four oceans. They had made a harpooner of him, and that barbed iron was in lieu of a scepter now."

The barbed iron of the harpoon was indeed a scepter of power. Melville understood that the harpoon was no small part of the attraction for the young Americans who converged the whaling waterfront of New Bedford, Massachusetts in the mid-19th century. Ishmael's friend Queequeg and other bronzed men from the seafaring islands of the South Pacific, reputed to be cannibals, rubbed shoulders on the docks with strapping lads from the New England frontier. Every week New Bedford absorbed "scores of green Vermonters and New Hampshire men, all a thirst for gain and glory in the fishery," said Ishmael. "They're mostly young, of stalwart frames, fellows who felled forests, and now seek to drop the axe and snatch the whale lance."

In the right hands, the harpoon was a source of wealth. Prosperous New Bedford was proof.

"But think not this famous town has only harpooners, cannibals, and bumpkins to show her visitors," Ishmael said. "... Nowhere in all America will you find more patrician lighthouses, parks and gardens more opulent than in New Bedford. Whence came they?"

From the wealth generated by whalers who had mastered the art of spearing fish, he said.

"Go and gaze upon the iron emblematic old harpoons round yonder lofty mansion," said Ishmael, "and your question will be answered. Yes, all these brave houses in the flowery gardens came from the Atlantic, Pacific, and Indian oceans. One and all, they were harpooned and dragged up of hither from the bottom of the sea."

With a harpoon a man might drag a fortune from the ocean. Or he might die.

Before shipping, out Ishmael and the other sailors attend a waterfront church service. The fire and brimstone preacher warns them to reconcile themselves to God, lest they meet an untimely fate at sea, which, statistically speaking, was not unlikely.

"Yes, it was the famous Father Mapple, so called by the whale men, among whom he was a very great favorite," said Ishmael. "He had been a sailor and in a harpooner in his youth, but for many years past dedicated his life to the ministry." From the pulpit, he preached about the biblical tale of Jonah, the sinner swallowed by a whale who repents in the belly of the beast. God hears his prayers and the fish vomits him out on the shore so that Jonah may live to serve God. The harpooners lived in a fearsome world.

The harpoon was, above all, a weapon. As the sailors in *Moby Dick* check into their boarding house, the night before heading out to sea, the mistress of the hotel demands Queequeg surrender his harpoon. She allowed none on the premises, she said.

"Why not?" asks Ishmael. "Every true whale man sleeps with his harpoon."

"Because it's dangerous," she said. Three years before, she explained, a young guest was murdered on the premises with a harpoon. "Ever since then I allow no boarders to take such a weapons in their rooms at night. So Mr. Queequeg (for she had learned his name), I will just take this here iron, and keep it for you till the morning." And so she did.

Ishmael and Queequeg go on to serve under the mad Captain Ahab, who drives his ship and crew to chase the elusive great white whale, Moby Dick, which escapes time and again. Melville's tale gave birth to an American myth of obsessive pursuit. The harpoon can do that to a man.

And then came industrialized fishing, and the harpoon was suddenly defunct. Within a few decades of *Moby Dick*, men like Captain Ahab had given way to the sea captains who served as foremen. With vast fortunes to be made, the whaling boats were transformed into factories of the sea, which harvested the waters of every kind of fish with giant nets and powerful guns. By the end of the 19th century, the harpooners were no more.

THE WHALE FISHERY.

Boat fastened to whale by harpoon and line; killing the whale with bomb-lance.   (Sect. v, vol. ii, pp. 45, 262, 267.)

From painting by J. S. Ryder.

Image ID: figb0201, NOAA's Historic Fisheries Collection Credit:

NOAA National Marine Fisheries Service

Yet the harpoon never went away, never even changed that much. The harpoon remains, as in the days of Poseidon, a sturdy staff, ten to fourteen feet long, with a bladed brass dart mounted on it, and a fishing line attached (and these days, an electric wire). In New England, the harpoon pole was two-inch thick oak shaft. More recently, the aluminum pole, one inch in diameter, has replaced oak, because it pierces the water better. Either way, oak or aluminum, the harpooner must hoist a thirty to fifty pound spear and hurl it at a fish speeding through the waves.

Here and there, in isolated places like the coast of Maine, where the livelihood of fishing was eternal and the "progress" represented by industrialized fishing was distant, the pastime of harpooning not only survived, but endured and spread throughout the 20th century. The elemental struggle of men and the sea, of hunting giant fish with a simple spear, never ceased to captivate daring men and curious boys.

I know because I was one of them.

Six in the boat I was hooked, shaped my whole life.
Photo from McIntire Family

1.

Boy

I did not come from a fisherman's stock. I was born and raised in the Berkshire Mountains in Massachusetts. In the mid-1960s, my father took our family to Maine when I was around five years old, and it was then I knew how I would spend my life.

We were in the harbor of Perkins Cove, Maine, and I loved the boats. It was getting dark. My dad had been trying for an hour to get me into the car, but another boat was coming in, and this one was different. They had to lift that crazy drawbridge-I'd never seen one of those-so the boat could get to the dock. I saw two kids on the boat about my age. I pulled out of my father's hand. I crawled though a sea of tourist legs, to the edge of that bait dock, and there I saw my first bluefin tuna.

Actually, I saw six of them. They were huge beyond even the imagination of my active five-year-old mind. I could not even breathe. I looked up to see one of those two kids looking at me from the roof of that boat. His brother joined him as they climbed onto the bait dock. The two boys helped run the hoist for their father. Soon those six gigantic fish were lying side by side. By now, I was covered in tuna blood and slime. It was the sweetest smell in the world.

I never spoke to those two boys that day. I remember feeling I was not worthy of them. I was learning the meaning of jealousy, envy, and shyness. But I knew there was no way in the world that I was not getting in on this! Those two boys were Billy and Bobby McIntire and the father was Sonny. They became my best friends growing up and their father, Sonny, even today is my hero for showing me the world I love, and so much more.

2.

The Magnificent Bluefin

A long, long time ago, the bluefin tuna, numbering in the tens of thousands, swam north in the Gulf Stream every spring. The fish, most of them eight to ten feet long and weighing in excess of eight hundred pounds, were hungry. They had spent the winter in the deep waters of the Gulf of Mexico where they spawned, using up the fat stored from their previous summer in Maine. They instinctively knew where they could find oil-rich herring needed to replenish their body fat. After the females released their eggs into the Gulf, they grouped in the deep water off the Florida Keys and found the strong currents of the Gulf Stream, which propelled their migration north.

This body of fish, the grandest of the species, blew right on by the lesser schools of their kind, as they traveled north. They stayed deep in the dark waters, never slowing nor sleeping, driven only by their quest for herring. They had no enemies. No man or creature was large or fast enough to catch them, especially when they stayed within the school forming an impenetrable mass. Years of survival and adaptation had taught them well. They stayed together, traveling in the Gulf Stream for two full days, only breaking away off the coast of New York to enter the colder waters of the North Atlantic

Now they reveled in the warmer surface water and light of the spring sun. Sensing their journey was nearing its end, they entered the deep waters of the Wilkerson Basin, passing other bluefin coming from the Georges Bank into the Bay of Cape Cod. They did not mix with these fish, ignoring them as they continued north.

Between the Jeffreys Bank and Platts Bank off the coast of southern Maine, the fish turned towards shore. Their feeding grounds were just a few miles ahead. There they found a huge biomass of herring and tore into them with ravenous appetite borne of privation. They feasted on herring till their bulging stomachs could hold no more. Content to be home, the fish turned back into the deeper waters, breaking up into smaller groups. The now-lazy fish swam with their backs out of the water digesting their first meal in weeks.

Aerial of 12 giants. Photo from Davis

3.

Maggie

So when I first encountered bluefin as a boy in the 1960s, I called them the Small Point Fish, in honor of the town near where they gathered annually. Now a half-century later, I'm tied to a dock in South West Harbor in Maine, and I believe I am seeing the descendants of those same fish. The barometric pressure is low and only a hand-full of boats are on the water. The bluefin could be gone in a day. Or they might tarry a little while longer.

How do I know they are the same fish as I saw in my youth? By their size. The Small Point Fish were massive and so are these guys

What is it about these magnificent fish that has captivated me for most of my life? For one thing, *they know.* They now know we are here, hunting them. As they migrate today, they know the noise of boats, the shadows they cast, the sound of the birds that follow, and the threat all of these signals represent. They know the surface of these waters is not a place to rest, to sleep, or to dream.

The bluefin are wise and wary. While plunging into deep water, they clean their gills. On the surface, the low pressure on the surface relaxes their skin and makes digesting sand eels and herring more enjoyable. The slack water of the afternoon makes the fish happy-yet they must always watch behind them.

They know that we, the men with harpoons, will try to approach them from behind. They know to never swim in a single direction. When a hunter boat approaches, they know where safety can be found: go deep, and fast. They know the boats around here do not release the bluefin back to the school as they do up North in Canada. The hunter boats kill fast, and sometimes all the fish in the group feel the pain of the harpoon's electric shock.

Now the great school of bluefin mostly stays away from the old feeding grounds near the Maine coast. They know a certain bay, far to the north, in Canadian waters, is not dangerous. Only occasionally will the school feel the need to revisit the feeding grounds of the past. They know this new bay is safe, a new bay of plenty. Up there the boats feed the school. They do not destroy it. Up there man is not a harsh hunter. Soon the bluefin passing the Maine coast will disappear from these waters to make the last leg of their migration to the bay up north.

And still we pursue them.

In the summer of 2016 I spent three weeks on my boat, the *Maggie,* looking for the bluefin with friend and boat mate Bradley. We had yet to see a running, or even a milling, tuna fish.

I looked over in the tower from which Bradley was scanning the waters and steering the boat. Neither of us stepped foot onto the pulpit in over two weeks.

Bradley knew what I was thinking.

"God hates you," he says.

I just nodded my head and looked harder. When darkness fell, our tired eyes were practically hanging on our cheeks. We descended from our perches for a late meal. Over beers, we talked about the fish, the bluefin.

How can a fish--a damn fish!-get into the very souls of men like us? How did they become a driving passion?

It *is* a puzzle. Bradley is happily married to a beautiful woman. He has children and dogs that love him. He leaves it all behind to spend countless hours every summer in a boat with me, the homeliest of company, and for very little money.

Bradley, like myself, has been bitten by these fish. Like Orlando Wallace and Carl McIntire, the old-timers who showed me the way, we are consumed by, and passionate about, these fish, often at our own expense. My God, I have less than a couple thousand dollars in operation funds in my account, and I'm still hoping for one good weather day to bail out the disappointing harpoon season of 2016.

In our hunt for the bluefin, Bradley and I splurged on hiring a pilot, Wayne Davies. We agreed to pay his fuel bill, which at five to six bucks a gallon, was large. His fuel bill for one day equaled our fuel tab for three days. It is money well spent-if you can put some fish on the deck.

We didn't catch up to the three bunches of fish that Wayne spotted that day. They were ten or twelve miles away from us. We went after them but the fish would settle before we arrived on the spot. This is common with bluefin. You need to be close by when they come up. By the end of the day our gamble did not pay off. The fish it turned out were sixty miles inshore. We missed them and so did Wayne. That said, having a world-class spotter pilot even for a day, can turn a season around. We just chose the wrong patch of water.

As harpooners we get used to that, searching sun up to sun down with little to show for it. But along the way, we encounter things that very few people will ever see for themselves. The oceans are a vast ecosystem that is best experienced while living on the water, sleeping far offshore in a thirty-six foot boat. It's not for everyone but the rewards are incredible.

The week before we saw a school of thousands of dolphins on the Georges Bank. What made this group special were the babies. Every female had a newborn swimming alongside of her. We watched hundreds of two-foot-long baby dolphins, speeding along with their wee little fins looking like wing-men in the Blue Angels fighter jets. They skimmed along, only inches from their moms in perfect formation. Bradley and I followed them for miles, amazed at the gift that had been bestowed on us. I get goose bumps thinking about it.

A sunfish swam right up to Bradley so close he could reach out and touch the creature from the deck. We met a leatherback turtle that would have climbed into our tuna door if we allowed it. A leaping minkie whale that was the happiest whale I have ever seen. He swam from out under our boat and launched for the heavens. We followed this guy for miles, cheering him on as he jumped to greater heights. He was playing with us, having fun with us, and we loved his company.

More often than not, each day on the water gives birth to a memory that will be implanted in my mind for the rest of my life.

Bradley making friends with a Sunfish. Photo from Decker

The livelihood of harpooning bluefin tuna has been transformed since I was a boy. I came of age "ironing the fish" before spotter planes and electric harpoons and I loved it. But as a young man I went to Alaska and launched a career in commercial fishing that took me around the world. I did not return to the harpoon fishery for decades, until I was in my fifties. Now my love of the bluefin is stronger than ever. Indeed, returning to the fishery has been life-changing for me.

I owe this re-birth to my wife, Maggie, who, bless her soul, has supported my crazy obsession with a smile, a shake of the head, and a twinkle in her eye. I am truly blessed, and you my dear reader, must take this advice from someone who has thrown many a harpoon. You cannot do it without a supporting network, from the fish buyer, to the boat mechanic to the first mate who makes it all possible. I am lucky to have a large network and it all begins with Maggie. My boat bears her name and my story is hers, too.

'Maggie' in Perkins Cove. Photo from Decker

4.

New Kids on the Pulpit

Age is a funny thing. I look at the black and white photographs of the harpooners, and I see today's old timers in their youth. I only need to look at a color photo of a skinny kid from forty years ago and then take a glance at the mirror to know I'm in the autumn years of my life. In fact, most of the old timers who built and handed down the harpooning tradition have gone on to chasing bluefin in the next world. Their sons and grandsons are following in their example, adopting and tweaking and often improving the techniques that were passed on to them.

Photo from Decker

Compared to the watercraft of twenty years ago-or a hundred years ago-the modern day harpoon boat is a very different animal. Today, we plough the Atlantic with electronically controlled diesel engines powering newly designed lightweight hulls at incredible speeds. The towers-our seat in the sky-are now made out of aircraft-grade aluminum. Thanks to the tensile strength the pulpits can hang out twenty feet or more off

9

the bow. The towers are higher and provide shade, an amenity unknown to us in our sun burnt youth. The younger generation is venturing out to harpoon the greatest fish in the sea in safer, better, faster boats than their fathers and grandfathers. They are also fishing a lot farther offshore, and they burn a lot less fuel doing it.

As in any endeavor from football to fishing, it is only natural that new young talent comes along to "retire" the old. If your son is way better at throwing the harpoon, then he is the guy to go out in the pulpit, and Dad drives the boat. Even the grand master of harpoon fishing, Sonny McIntire, now seventy-five years old, has taken the wheel, and his youngest son, Shane, does the throwing on most days.

We can see the new harpooners are extremely talented. They may be a bit more patient with their throws than we were at their age. Thanks to more effort and wiser fish, they have fewer good chances during the season. But they seem better at making each opportunity count.

Perkins Cove, a small harbor in Ogunquit Maine, is now three generations removed from the first days of the first harpoon men. Yet it is still renowned for having some of the best harpooners in the fishery. In fact, if you had to pick the ten best harpooners in the world, a couple of them would call Ogunquit home. Some have the famous last names of the profession like McIntire. Some are new. The best harpooner today in the Cove, Timmy Virgen, already has a place in the history book of harpooning.

In today's commercial fishing industry, the survival of such a century-old tradition is unusual, if not unique. The harpooners of Maine fiercely protect their beloved life-style and refuse to let it fade away. This is what makes the Cove fishermen so special.

Unfortunately the flip side of self-protection is jealousy, which means Perkins Cove today is not as friendly as it was in my youth. The Cove harpooners are very anti-plane. They think aerial assistance in tuna harpooning should be outlawed. Just a few years ago, it seems they all had planes, themselves. Now the harpooners who enlist the help of pilots are not welcome, and those who do, don't take the time to stop. There are too many other beautiful Maine ports to pull into for the night, and off load a fish. Sadly many boats now just avoid Perkins Cove.

The new talent pool in harpooning is found in Massachusetts. These days the Maine boats chase the Massachusetts boats instead of the other way around. The names may be new--Gibbs, Sullivan, and "Hollywood"--but they are the same breed as the men of Maine. Wherever it happens these days, it happens the same way. Talented individuals form teams and the spotter pilots lead the way.

In some ways, harpooning tuna a thoroughly modern activity. There are challenges unknown when I was coming up: state rules, federal regulations, international markets, and new technologies. Harpooning the bluefin has become a complex business enterprise than spans the globe.

At the same time, it is still a game of inches and pounds. To sell a bluefin today, the fish must measure at least seventy-three inches long. Now put yourself in the pulpit, the extended perch jutting out in front of a harpoon boat. You are coming up on a school of fish standing ten feet above the water, traveling at seven knots, and you must decide what is a seventy-three-inch keeper and what's a seventy-inch short and you have only a split second to make the decision: to throw or not. Just as Yogi Berra famously said, "How can you think and hit at the same time?" It is hard to think and harpoon at the same time. The thought process messes with your concentration.

The law now dictates that season does not start till June 1, regardless of how many fish are around in late May. Climate change affects the season too. In 2012 the water temperatures in the Gulf of Maine were very warm and the fish arrived early. By the opening bell of June, the huge majority of the fish had already moved on to Canadian waters. The second wave of fish that came that summer were mostly juveniles and shorts, which are unlawful to keep. Commercially, the year was a bust for all of the boats.

The harpooner of yesterday didn't think about such things. He just ironed the fish. Today, you have to have to have the latest technology just to keep up. That means you throw an electric harpoon.

Glen Perkins

Kurt Christinson. Photos from Decker

Jackie's boat '*The Susan*'.

The Gloucester gang, Greg Chorebanian. Photos from Decker

5.

Shocker

The electric harpoon, otherwise known as the shocker, has been around for a long time. Originally invented by RCA in the late 1950's for harpooning whales, the shocker found its way on board a bluefin tuna boat a few years later, thanks to man named Ed Gerry.

Born and bred in Down East Maine, Gerry was ahead of his time. He was a self-taught inventor with a genius-level IQ and he was known for thinking outside the proverbial box. When everybody was using converted lobster boats for harpooning tuna, Ed came up with a totally new design. In 1962, he ordered up a unique watercraft that he dubbed the *Scoot*, one of the first boats built and designed for the sole purpose of harpooning. Using a design similar to the popular Carolina sportfishing boats, he paid a Massachusetts company to construct a twin engine, gas-powered wooden boat, with a flared bow. The bow kept the waves away from the deck and the flying bridge gave the boat captain a better view of the water ahead. Such a design was common in sportfishing and unknown in harpoon boats. The *Scoot* was way ahead of her time.

When Ed Gerry saw the electric harpoon used by the multinational corporation RCA for killing whales, he adapted the idea for hunting the bluefin. RCA's system was powered by four huge eight volt, direct current (DC) batteries and a heavy copper wire carried the current to the harpoon. Gerry agreed to give the contraption a try.

The idea of using electricity to kill the tuna appealed to Gerry. Up until that time, harpoon fishermen simply "ironed" the fish with the dart of their harpoon and let the harpooned fish swim until it died. Rather than try and pull the fish in, they put out a floating flag, known as a "flag end." The flag marked the end of the line with the ironed fish. The harpooner could then resume hunting. When the flagged fish died, usually a few hours later, they returned to the flag and hauled in the catch.

This was the way harpooners had fished for years but Gerry saw the system was far from ideal. It required keeping track of numerous lines. The dying fish towed off the lines in totally different directions. The gear would sometimes get hung up on debris or rocks on the ocean floor. Lost flag ends were pretty common.

Gerry worked with the RCA system for the entire summer, learning its strengths and limitations. The biggest problem was that unit required the fisherman to keep the power on for upwards of sixty seconds after the fish had been harpooned. That's how long it took for the direct current to kill a fish weighing up to eight hundred pounds. Another problem was safety. When the unit was engaged it created one hell of an electric arc that could kill man just as easily as it could kill a fish.

Over the next few years Gerry fine-tuned the RCA electric harpoon, making it easier and safer to use. He caught a heap of tuna, and the shocker was born. The value of his innovation wasn't lost on other harpooners. One fisherman in the Gloucester area who took a keen interest in the shocker was Ed's good friend Fred Breed, an eye surgeon who owned a boat called the *Jaguar*. Breed installed a shocker and boated forty-three small fish out of one school. That was more fish than anyone thought possible.

Ed Gerry passed away in 1972, but his son Doug carried on with development of the electric harpoon. Using lessons learned from his father, Doug Gerry perfected today's modern electric harpoon, which is used on every harpoon boat in the industry. When Doug deployed the on-board batteries to generate an alternating current, instead of a direct currently, he discovered he only needed around forty or fifty volts to kill a fish. The AC harpooner was faster and more efficient than DC prototype.

Throughout the 1970's and 1980's Doug continued to tweak, experiment and fine-tune different power sources, always looking an improvement. The harpoon system he perfected had a five hundred-watt motor driven from a twelve-volt alternator. The resulting electrical pulse killed the fish almost instantly.

Today, Doug Gerry is a solar power expert. He can build you a home powered by the sun. You can also find him on Platts on a bluebird day in the summer. He still owns the *Scoot,* a boat now older than most of the fishermen who ride in it. She is still beautiful and still moored in, you guessed it, Perkins Cove, Maine.

In the 1980's Japanese fish buyers took notice of the quality of the fish Doug Gerry was delivering. In Japan, where sushi is a centerpiece of the national diet, the quality of tuna is a high priority for which people will pay dearly. And quality means knowing the fish.

Bluefin tuna fish are warm-blooded. Obtaining the best sashimi-grade tuna depends on how the fish is handled from the moment it is caught until the minute it is offloaded in Tokyo. The fish harpooned in pre-shocker days were simply left to bleed to death, a process that usually took hours. The whole time the fish was in pain and traumatized, with stress hormones surging through its muscles. All of which affected the quality of its flesh as food.

By contrast, a bluefin killed by an electric jolt doesn't even know what happened. One minute it is swimming about in the North Atlantic, and then-lights out. Just as the best venison in the world comes from a buck that is first dropped right in its tracks, not one that has been wounded or run hard by dogs, so the best tuna comes from fish killed by the electric harpoon.

The standards of the Tokyo market are demanding but rewarding: Kill the fish right and you might get paid fifty dollars a pound. Kill the fish wrong, you might be lucky to get a couple bucks a pound.

That's why every harpoon boat today has a version of Doug Gerry's shocker. With today's technology the electric harpoon is a very effective and lucrative instrument-if you have it hooked up right.

Jack on 'Cobra', 1974. Photo from Cadario Family

Last summer I rigged up a shocker system for my boat, the *Maggie*. I was relying on a drawing done by Bradley, who depicted an inverter that generated one hundred and twenty volts from a twelve-volt battery. When I tested the system at the dock it seemed to work fine, so we went fishing. Out on the water, we quickly realized something was not right. I ironed a fish and he swam away, very much alive. The shocker shocked but it did not kill that tuna or any other bluefin that day. We had to put out the old-fashioned flag ends to track our fish.

Back on shore, I told Sonny McIntire, veteran harpooner, about the problem. He said it sounded familiar.

"A few years ago a buddy hooked up a new shocker just like you," he recalled, "and he got the negative and positive wires out on the pulpit mixed up. When he harpooned a tuna and threw the switch, it would just piss off the fish, and they would really go! I think he was hitting them with twelve volts instead of a hundred and twenty".

Sonny had himself a good laugh about that damn fool.

No way I could have done something so dumb, I thought.

But I did. I had the hot wire going to the grounding plate and the negative run out on the stand. A little mistake cost me a big fish.

The throwing line most guys use today is much lighter than the line first used by Ed Gerry in the early versions of the shocker. Today's line, running from sixty to a hundred feet long, is a multi-strand wire, 12- or 14-gauge. The more strands, the better throwing lines coils up. The wire is threaded through Samson braid, a quarter or three-eighths inch line. The harpooner will either hold the coil in his left hand (if he is right handed) or keep the line coiled up in a bucket by his side.

The "hot button" (also known as the mash button) delivers the electric jolt. The location of the button varies with the boat. Some guys rig up the button on the pulpit from which they throw the harpoon. If the harpoon strikes the fish, they mash the button, sending the juice.

Other boats have the button in the tower. That way the guy with the best view of the fish hits the switch. He just better not hit that button while you are holding that pole. The harpoon, when charged, is a deadly weapon, especially in a water-filled environment. I know one harpooner whose shocker had a faulty solenoid; the current knocked him right out of the boat and he had to be plucked out of the water.

In short, the shocker is a good friend that has to be handled with care. Just like a spotter pilot.

My favorite '*Scoot*'photo from Decker

I never got to know Doug Gerry until my second round of tuna fishing in my fifties, but I knew of Dougie since I was just a little kid. He had the shocker, kept the blue boat down in Beverly. Jackie Stewart fished with him along with David Tasey, (who would later fly for him) and even Rickie, Cadario's mate. Doug caught a heap of bluefin back in the 1970's.

The Scoot Too was probably one of the most famous of those classic Royal boats, you knew it was the Scoot from a long ways off...

Doug still owns the boat, she can been found in Perkins Cove, Maine. I tip my hat to you Sir Doug, you sir have done right.

TOURNAMENT PREVIEW — This 758-pound bluefin was one of eight brought to the dock yesterday and 10 brought in Saturday. In on the catch off Bailey Island were, from left, David Taisey, "Scrunch" (the only way he would identify himself), and Doug Gerry of the "Scoot Too" from Beverly, Mass. The Casco Bay Tuna Tournament starts tomorrow and a clambake is scheduled at 4 p.m. today at Mackerel Cove Beach. This year's tournament is expected to be the biggest yet after a story about the annual affair appeared recently in the New York Times. (Don Hinckley photo)

Ed Gerry (Doug's Dad). Photo from Gerry

Old style stuff...flag end barrel that we used to tie to a harpooned fish so we could find them, while we hunted down the next one. 1930-1940's era.

Harpoon darts. Photos from Decker

6.

Spotter Planes

Spotter planes have been used in fishing for a long time. In the seine fishery, where boats cast vast nets, planes can make a huge difference. The planes can tell the boats where to set their nets and when to pull them in, wrapping up a whole school of fish in one swoop.

By contrast, planes were seldom used in the early days of harpoon fishing. There were so many tuna and they were so unwary the added cost of a plane was unnecessary. That began to change in the mid-1980's as the number of boats chasing the tuna multiplied, while the legal limits on catching did not change much. With the increased competition, spotter planes came into demand.

The mid-1980s was when I was fishing in Alaska and then the South Seas, so I missed what turned out to be the heyday of the spotter plane. I just heard the stories from my buddies in Maine, and they told a story of a new level of harpooning.

The good pilots demanded top pay and got it. The going rate for spotting bluefin was a meaty third of the value of the catch. Who could blame them?

Spotting bluefin from a Piper Super Cub while five hundred feet over the water is no easy task. A lot of the planes had long-range belly tanks enabling them to stay in the air for hours. That meant the pilots had to maintain concentration, hour after hour, looking out for both fish and other planes.

Spotting tuna can be dangerous. Many pilots don't want to fly over the water near shore, never mind thirty to fifty miles from the beach. If you get into any kind of trouble and have to put down, you're going in the drink and planes don't float worth beans. The skies can be crowded, too. It isn't uncommon to have six or eight planes spotting fish in the same area.

Pilots are demanding. Just like the harpooners, spotter pilots are a unique breed with high expectations. You had better hit what fish they spot or else you're not going to have a pilot. The pilots hate missed fish probably more than the guy throwing the pole.

From the late 1980's to the early 2000's spotter pilots were essential to harpooners. Just about every boat or network of boats, had a plane in the air helping them. The harpoon quota was filled quickly. Everyone needed a second boat in the general category to catch more fish before the season was ended by law. Working with a plane increased the catch.

When the price of fuel started to climb, the boat owners found themselves in a catch-22. They were paying 35 percent of the value of the catch to the pilot and another 25 percent to the mate. With the remainder, the owner had to cover the fuel bill, insurance, mooring, and maybe a boat payment. Every boat had to make a difficult decision: catch less fish without a plane and keep more of the money, or catch a lot more and pay a lot more.

The majority of the pilots either abandoned the business or priced themselves right out of the game. Today there are probably fewer than a dozen planes flying full time in the bluefin harpoon fishery, although those planes catch the majority of the quota each summer.

The competition between the plane and the non-plane boats generates jealousy. When the guys with the planes hear bitching from the non-plane boats, they just shrug it off. "Hire a plane then," is their standard reply. In response, the guys who find their own fish unaided talk about outlawing the damn planes.

To me there's no reason to bitch, just make a choice. Either pay the pilot, and hope to catch twice as many fish (you'll get a heap more opportunities), or live or die by your own eyesight. You had best be ready to look real hard all summer long.

I returned to the fishery full bore in 2015, my first season with my new boat, the *Maggie.* I never had a plane all season long, not even for a single day. Now I think about damn planes twenty four-seven.

The truth is that deploying a plane is the only way to go if you want to catch a lot of bluefin. It's not a coincidence that very best harpooner today, just so happens to have the very best spotter pilot in the business. Sean Sullivan, captain of the *Back Off*, and his pilot, Norman St. Pierre have been working together for more than twenty years. In 2015 Norman told me they harpooned ninety-one fish. That was more bluefin than all the non-plane southern Maine boats combined (mine included) caught all summer.

One of my best friends is Jerry Fraser, publisher of *National Fisherman* magazine. He is an aviation instructor, and experienced airman. When I talk to Jerry about the spotter business he just shakes his head and laughs. To be a successful spotter pilot, he says, you need huge brass balls. You need to throw out everything you have been taught about safety and have no fear. Spotter pilots are the base jumpers, cliff divers, or extreme skiers of the aviation world. How do you train somebody to have no fear? You don't.

Spotter pilots are born, not taught, and they're not born very often.

To find a pilot I would have to advertise in a newspaper or fishing magazine with a pitch like this:

"Wanted: Small plane pilot for seasonal work in New England fishery; opportunity for good gross income."

Now if that's all I wrote, I would probably be buried with responses. But, to be honest, I would have to provide some relevant details, such as:

"Must have good eyes, experience preferred; Must own a high-wing single engine, preferably a Super Cub with a belly tank."

Now that might attract a few responses, but to be totally honest, I would also have to say:

"Must put in six hours of airtime, eight if possible, every day all summer long; Must be willing to fly over Georges Bank in late season. You get a third of the gross; pay all your expenses."

I don't think I would get many calls.

Why do I want a spotter pilot to work with me on the *Maggie*?

If I try to sneak up on a bluefin, the creature knows just what I am trying to do. The advantage is always with the fish. This wasn't so fifty years ago, before the fish learned fully what a harpoon boat was. Today, the fish are extremely wary and the boats with planes have a huge advantage. The planes are able to cover large swathes of ocean locating fish and providing co-ordinates to the boat. The best three harpooners have three of the best pilots flying for them.

Mark Brochu is the pilot for Bill Muniz, known as "Hollywood." On the backside of Cape Cod in June 2015, a handful of boats and a couple planes were chasing fish that were running shy and deep. I had two shots and missed both times. One fish, swimming eight feet below the surface, left such a tiny wake. The large number in the bunch (fifty or more) made it impossible to approach the lagging fish. I was getting busted before I could have any kind of throw. I had nothing.

Meanwhile, Mark was watching from five hundred feet up and he could see the lagging fish. He was lining up Hollywood a half mile behind these herds and riding him right up the last ones. I have no idea how many fish those guys caught that day but it was lot more than I did. I steamed my boat ten miles away just so I didn't have to watch.

I have never met Sean Sullivan but I speak with his pilot Norman quite often. We sell our fish to the same company in Chatham Massachusetts. They have a truck waiting for the *Back Off* in Chatham all summer to take their catch to market. That alone tells the story of their success.

The third top harpooner in the world is Greg Gibbs from Green Harbor,

Massachusetts. Greg has been in the stand since he was fourteen years old, and he too relies on a spotter plane most of the time. That doesn't mean he isn't a great harpooner. I have never fished with him, but I have witnessed a couple of the hardest shots I think I have ever seen. I had Sonny McIntire with me and he and I ironed one fish. I think Greg got three. So I have one of the greatest harpooners that ever drew a breath on my boat, and Greg took us to school.

It was impressive. We came upon a big milling bunch of fish, three hundred or more in the herd. The fish came to the surface and swam in big arcs. The sea was so rough you could only get out on the pulpit while going down wind. Greg went out and I saw him throw thirty feet or more at fish with their backs out of the water in six foot seas--and he hit them. Now, I'm a pretty good harpooner, but I could not have made that throw if my life depended on it. He did it twice!

And that day, he did it without a spotter plane. So technology is important but it isn't everything. It certainly wasn't in the early days of harpooning.

Photo from Gibbs

Spotter Pilot Mark Brochu

Hollywood of Wicked Tuna. Photos from Brochu

BOOK II
YESTERDAY

7.

Orlando Wallace

No one can say for sure what year it was but everyone agrees Orlando Wallace was the first American to ever harpoon a bluefin tuna. Born in 1889, Orlando was a lobsterman in Small Point, Maine who got bored with pulling traps and decided to try something different. That was Orlando's way.

Orlando was an unusual man. He was all of eleven years old when he told his father he was going to sea on one of the salt-cod boats that worked the Maine coast. His father told him he was too young to be a dory fisherman. The young man (yes, he was a man at eleven; no one who goes to sea is a boy) told his father he was going anyway. His dad told him not to come back home if he did. Orlando never looked back.

On the salt cod boats, young Orlando learned the ways of the trade. The boatmen went out on a big schooner for four to six weeks a time. Each ship had a bunch of dories-rowboats really. The dories went out from the mother ship to set two or three taut lines (or tub trawls) with a hundred hooks or so per trawl. These lines, hauled in by hand from the dory. At the time the boats only put up the codfish. Everything else they caught was tossed back-haddock, pollock, even halibut-because, unlike cod, they could not be cured by salting.

The captain of Orlando's boat was particular about size of the cod too. He instructed the crew to put on cut bait-small offerings of herring-to target the market size cod: not too big, not too small. The dories would return to the mother ship in the afternoons and unload the day's catch to be split, salted and stacked in the salt hold.

Before long, young Orlando was in trouble with the captain. He wanted to catch the biggest fish, so he waited until the captain was out of sight and put a whole herring on the hook. Orlando caught a lot of halibut, which they could not sell, but he loved eating them and had bragging rights of catching the largest fish. The captain chided his youngest crew member but Orlando never shook his big-fish syndrome.

And so he came of age on the water. In those days it wasn't unusual for a young man to go to sea at an early age and stay there. I doubt Orlando Wallace ever finished 7th grade.

One fine Maine summer morning, it might been 1909 or 1910 or 1911 (the dates varied depending on the teller of the tale) , Orlando had enough of pulling lobster traps. He decided he would go and try to harpoon a swordfish, which was also unusual. The swords were big and slow and they liked to bask in the sun on the surface of the water. So he thought he might boat one. But there weren't (and aren't) a lot of swordfish in the waters off Maine. And they don't swim in schools. When you see a swordfish, it is usually alone. But Orlando did see bluefin tuna everywhere, so he started chasing them. He managed to iron one of them and began to search for another.

The details are lost to history but knowing Orlando's upbringing I imagine he might have told the story of his first harpooning expedition in the style of Marshall Dodge, a popular Maine comedian in the 1950s and 1960s. Using a character named "Bert" as his foil, Dodge affectionately spoofed the laconic style favored by the "Down East" fishermen as they plied their trade.

Here's how Marshall Dodge, as "Bert," might have told the tale:

"Bert," Orlando says, "the lobsters have not started the shed yet. Let's go see if we can find one of those swords in the deep water?"

Bert flicked the oak trap off the rail.
"Yep," he grinned. "Fresh swordfish steaks for Sunday church lunch, the missus will be pleased."

The two fishermen jogged off to the east a few miles. The ocean was as flat and greasy calm as a mill pond. Not a breath of air stirred the blue green waters of the North Atlantic. Just a few miles out, in an area that cod fisherman call "The Kettle," the sea floor drops away to almost a hundred fathoms, meaning six hundred feet. Here the swordfish would come in search of squid mixed in with the vast herring biomass around the

Kettle. On calm days the swordfish could be occasionally be seen surfacing to bask in the July sun.

The two men stacked up some totes, the wood boxes used to hold caught lobsters, to gain a bit of height on their open deck double-ender. Offshore in the deep water they could see the abundant horse mackerel plowing about, leaving great big boiling wakes all over the water's surface.

Orlando just sat on the rail shaking his head,

"Bert," he says, "I'm sorry this was just a total waste of time. The damn tuna fish are plowing the ocean to a whitewater froth. Everywhere I look there's another bunch. There won't be a swordfish within a hundred miles of here. A damn fish couldn't find a peaceful place to lay about without getting run down by a thousand pound mackerel!"

"You ain't kidding," Bert says grabbing Orlando by the collar and yanking him up onto the totes. "Hop up here a second and take a look at size of these cows. Look at that bunch of monsters. There must be fifty of them. I'll drive. You throw."

"What? At one of those?" Orlando says looking at the tuna. "Have you been into your fathers apple jack again? What will we do if we hit one? They're as big as basking sharks!"

Bert shrugs his shoulders and lines up on the end of the bunch,

"I got color on them," he says. "You better hurry."

Orlando, still mumbling, picks up the ten foot oak pole and a hand full of throwing line.

Standing in the bow, Orlando throws the harpoon, which catches of the monster tuna fish right behind the dorsal fin. The fish starts thrashing, smashing the wooden pole as it blasts off towards the bottom.

"How much line you say was on that coil?" Orlando yells as he watches the line peel overboard.

"I don't know, fifty fathoms maybe," Bert says, jumping off the boxes to help. "Get the flag end ready."

"What's a flag end?" Orlando asks with a hurt expression.

"I just invented them," Bert says. "In the meantime just cleat off the end and hold on. We are about to go for a ride old boy!"

The two men are off to what New England whalers called "a Nantucket sleigh ride." For an hour that feels like eternity, the mighty fish does its damnedest to pull their skiff under the water whilst towing them here and there and everywhere. Eventually their prayers, creatively embellished with a variety of curse words, are answered and the fish dies.

They pull the fish back to the boat, hand over hand, being careful to not to "pull a dart"-let the harpoon slip out and lose the fish.

They get in to the harbor around midnight. They wreck the bait dock's winch attempting to hoist the mammoth fish out of the boat. Finally they get a couple of block and tackles set up. A couple of hours later, the fish is on the dock, but kind of beat up.

"I don't think we can ship this one to Japan, not yet," Bert says. "We'll need to develop those markets first. So you might as well just cut it up for lobster bait."
"We got good sticking weather the next few days, so screw the lobsters," he goes on. "See ya in the morning. One more thing, we are harpooners now so, we don't have to leave till eight."

Bert leaves.
"Oh yeah, nice fish," he yells over his shoulder, leaving Orlando straddling the fish covered in sweat and tuna blood.
That's the story of how Orlando Wallace became a harpooner.

The next spring Orlando Wallace and his brother Amos were out on the water, sitting on the rail of their lobster boat, all smiles. They were watching the first feeding bluefin of the summer who paid no attention to their small boat. The arrival of the tuna fish in late May signaled the start of the summer season, promising the young men a blessed break from hauling lobster gear. The harsh winter months were now behind them. It was harpoon time again.

The tuna were feasting on the herring in only eighty feet of water, the eight hundred pound fish exploding out of the water to gulp down fish as a cloud of birds hovered over them swooping in for scraps. The show lasted for around thirty minutes and when it was over the fishermen went back to hauling their pots.

Back at the dock all the lobstermen could talk about was the tuna. They had all seen them, even more than the summer before when Orlando and Amos brought that first fish to the dock. Now all the Small Point lobstermen were going after them. They had spent the winter rigging their boats with pulpits, made from the finest oak planks from which they could spot the tuna. No one in Small Point slept much that night in anticipation of chasing the giants. This year was going to be special.

The harpooning way of life had been revived. The world of Moby Dick was gone. The bluefin had replaced the whales as prey. But the questing spirit of the harpooners lived on.

Orlando Wallace, 1859-1918.

Photo from

McIntire Family

8.

Carl McIntire

Every so often someone is born in this world who makes a real difference in the lives of many people. Carl McIntire was one of these people. Like Orlando Wallace, Carl was born and raised in Small Point, Maine. A hundred years ago there were three families in Small Point-the Wallace's, the Gilliam's, and the McIntire's-who started it all. Orlando Wallace, Oscar Gilliam and Carl McIntire are the forefathers of all bluefin harpoon fishermen today.

Orlando passed on what he knew to Carl, and Carl passed it on to me and countless others. He gave so many of us a simple but amazing gift: he took us fishing.

Carl McIntire was born in 1916 one of two brothers born to Raymond McIntire, a merchant marine officer. Raymond would only sail as mate, because he made almost the same amount of money as the captain, but did not have to shoulder the full responsibility of the ship. Gone to sea for extended periods of time, Raymond left his two sons, Carl and Herbert, in charge of the household chores and helping their mother. At a very early age, the two brothers went lobstering. In the summers, they were harpooners and they learned the art from Orlando Wallace.

As Carl came of age in the 1930s, the harpooners of Small Point fine-tuned their technique. They fitted their open deck lobster boats with short masts topped with a crow's nest so they could see the fish better. When lobster boats with a small house were introduced, they stood on the roof.

Harpooning was not difficult. The fish were easy to approach and to iron. Orlando developed the device of the "flag end,"-a bamboo pole attached to a weighted buoy, with a bright colored flags tied to the high end. The flag end marked a line that had a captured fish. When the fish were thick in numbers, the Small Point men would have thirty or forty flags going before they hauled the giants in.

It was not a lucrative business. When shipped to the Boston market, the tuna fish sold for just a few cents a pound. The bluefin were sometimes smoked and canned. Early on, their oil was used in lamps, but most often the fish were ground up for pet food and fertilizers. The Small Point harpooners made up for the low price with a large volume of fish. Some of the tuna they brought in weighed up to a thousand pounds each.

Life was good in Small Point. By the end of the 1930s, the Great Depression was ending, new boats were being built, and most everyone was prospering. The war raging over in Europe was thousands of miles away and it felt like it. But when the Japanese bombed Pearl Harbor on December 7th ,1941, everything changed.

Raymond McIntire was assigned to work on the Liberty ships, transporting men and war material to the Europe. Herbie McIntire joined the Navy. The price of bluefin went up to ten cents a pound, as tuna was suddenly in demand to feed the American soldiers heading off to Europe and Asia. In addition, commercial fishermen served as a home defense force, keeping an eye on coastal waters for foreign intruders.

The war didn't stop Carl McIntire from harpooning or taking young people out on his boat. Once the war got going in Europe, the only bodies available were children. So in the summer of 1942, Carl had room on his brand new boat, the *Priscilla Cameron*, for fourteen-old Merle Gilliam, son of his neighbor Oscar. Full of teenage rebellion Merle jumped from his father's boat to fish with Carl in the summer of 1942. They caught forty-four fish.

Unfortunately, his dad landed more than a hundred. That winter young Merle hounded his father to let him back on the boat. Dad let the message soak in-the grass isn't always greener, and all that-but he let him come him back. With the war in full swing, young Merle Gilliam started making real money.

In 1944 Oscar paid him ten percent of the value of every bluefin they caught, which averaged out to about five dollars per fish, a hell of a lot of dough for a teenager in those days. They landed one hundred and ten fish, and Merle saved more than two thousand dollars that summer.

The next summer, the fish returned to Small Point in ever-larger numbers. After they had some luck in the June, Merle told his dad he had heard one of their neighbors, Norm Bracket, a seine fisherman, had tried harpooning near Seal Island and missed twenty eight times. Norm was lousy with a harpoon but it sounded like he had found a huge school. Soon the Gilliams' boat, *Mina B*, was steaming at top speed for Seal Island.

They found tuna swarming in big clusters with fifty or more fish in each herd. Oscar and Merle chased fish till darkness fell. When the last one hit the deck, the wooden rails of *Mina B* were almost level with the bloody water around them. They had boated twelve fish, all of them monsters; a six hundred pound fish was one of the smaller ones. That was the most bluefin anyone had ever caught in one day, a record that was destined to be broken.

Back at the dock Oscar Gilliam sold forty four hundred pounds of dressed out tuna at twelve cents a pound. He wound up with five hundred and fifty dollars cash in his hand. It was the most money Merle had ever seen in his life. His dad peeled off a fifty-dollar bill and handed it him. Merle stared at that fifty for a minute while doing the math. Then he held his hand out to his father for the five dollars still owed. Merle knew what he was going to do, he was going to buy his own boat.

Carl McIntire taking kids fishing, 1940.

Photo from McIntire Family

Carl McIntire with a boat load of cove rats, 1980-1982 era.

Photo from McIntire Family

9.

First Throw

In those days, Priscilla McIntire often served as Carl's stern man in the boat that bore her name. She drove the boat up on the fish and Carl ironed them. When their son, Carl Junior, known as "Sonny," was born in 1940, Priscilla had to take a few days off, but she was soon back on board with a small bundle wrapped in her arms. Every time Carl would harpoon a fish, the baby would cry. It was the excitement, his mother said. You could say, without exaggeration, Sonny McIntire was born to be a harpooner.

The first time Carl allowed Sonny to throw was when he was ten years old. It was the summer of 1950 and the Small Point fish were back in large numbers from the Cod Ledge to the Kettle. Across that twenty miles of water, the fish were going wild feeding on herring. Ten-year-old Sonny steered the boat into the feeding fish while Carl threw. But the father kept missing. He finally asked Sonny if he would like to take a crack at one.

Would he? Sonny had been waiting for the chance. He had practiced by climbing a tree in their backyard and throwing a rake handle at a board nine inches across-his estimate of the span between dorsal fin and tail on a bluefin. If he could hit that board he could hit a tuna fish, or so he thought.

Sonny grabbed the oak pole harpoon. It was so heavy that he had to choke up, as he did with his bat in Little League baseball. He saw three fish staying up in the water, giving him a target. He threw at the one closest to him. The harpoon skimmed by its side but missed. He would not get another chance to throw for two more summers.

He needed more practice, Carl said. That fall Sonny's parents built a porch on the back of the house, and it was the perfect height to practice from. Sonny didn't have to climb the tree any more. He armed himself with multiple "harpoons:" a leftover broom, a headless rake, a stray shovel handles, or better yet a real oak harpoon that had fractured and was no longer usable.

That missed fish haunted Sonny. He threw and threw vowing to not to miss again, if his dad would just give him another chance. While other kids where playing baseball, or building tree houses and forts, Sonny would be throwing off that porch till his arms ached. Sonny would be out back practicing after dark and Carl and Priscilla would have to order him to come inside for bed. It was years before the McIntire's had a lawn again. The whole back yard was covered in divots. Harpooning was all Sonny thought about.

The post-war years were good for the McIntire's. Herbie came back from the war. Both he and Carl had new boats, built for lobstering but primarily for harpooning. Herbie's was called the *Hazel A*, and Carl's the *Priscilla Cameron*. Those boats were seen from Cape Cod to way Down East. Wherever the tuna fish were running thickest, the McIntire's were not far away.

But the fish were not coming back to Small Point as they had in years past. Those fish were giants, the latest generation in an ancient bloodline. Warm blooded and intelligent, they were learning what danger lurked in those waters. An eight hundred pound bluefin might be thirty, forty or fifty years old. An animal does not live so long by being dumb. After years of getting chased around the rocky shores of mid-coast Maine, the fish had moved on.

They started gathering more than fifty miles south around Boon Island, a cluster of rocks topped with the tallest lighthouse in New England, built in 1811.

There were all kinds of stories about Boon Island, from tales of pirates who took refuge there in the 18th century to rumors of Nazi submarines that lurked nearby during the war. But it was the tuna that attracted Carl.

Over the course of five or six years, the bluefin started gathering there every summer, and the harpooners followed. The body of fish Carl and others found around Boon Island was amazing. The fishermen would only work on the fringes of these schools, bringing in plenty of fish while seeing four or five bunches more running at the same time. This had not happened around Small Point in years. At night Carl had a long ride home.

Carl had met Leon Perkins and Billy Tower, a couple of fishermen, also harpooners, who lived in the town of Ogunquit on Perkins Cove, a small protected inlet, only eight miles from Boon Island. Around 1950 Carl started to use the Cove as an outpost, a home away from home. In 1952, he decided to move his family there.

Ogunquit Harbor Master Fred Mayo's grandmother, estimated 1940

Photo from Mayo

Carl and Sonny McIntire,
1964.
Photo from McIntire Family

10.

The Cove

Carl and Priscilla McIntire bought a century-old home in Ogunquit, and Sonny, now twelve, was glad to move. He only cared that they were closer to the tuna fish. He would have lived on Boon Island if he had to.

It took a measure of courage it took to relocate in those days. The families of the Maine coast had deep roots with generations of living in one place. The normal thing to do was to stay put. An outsider coming in was not welcome. Carl found someone had cut the lines to his lobster traps. He was in hostile territory.

But fishermen, by nature, are explorers, especially harpooners who are both fishermen and hunters. From the beginning of human history, hunters have moved around. If you compared Maine to the Stone Age, you could say the McIntire's were like the Stone Age hunter-gatherers of Siberia, who walked across the land bridge to North America and discovered a new world. They moved to Perkins Cove and found a new world of harpooning.

Merle Gilliam probably would have followed Carl if the Korean War hadn't erupted. Merle had married his childhood sweetheart, June McIntire, Carl's youngest sister, and they started a family. In the summers of the late 1940s, his boat, the *Dottie G*, was often tied up next to Carl's in Perkins Cove. He even tried to buy a small house on the Cove but in the end the old woman who owned the house did not sell. I think she was a Perkins and didn't care for outsiders either.

Merle Gilliam was drafted into the Army and had to go serve in Germany. Merle and June's second child, Michael, was born when Merle was going though basic training. He would not see the boy until he returned home a year later. When he returned, he decided to stay in Small Point.

Herbie McIntire decided to stay in Small Point, too. Despite their passion for harpooning, lobstering remained their chief source of income.

Besides, once Carl moved to Perkins Cove, the whole clan had a place to go during the summer harpooning season. Carl McIntire was leading the way.

On the surface, Boon Island is just an ugly cluster of granite boulders covered in seaweed and seagull shit. Aside from the lighthouse, its only redeeming feature is that it serves as rookery for harbor seals. But the rocky island lies atop a sea mount, an underwater mountain with only the very top breaking the surface.

A few miles east lies Boon Island Ledge, another sea mount that does not quite make it to the surface, but breaks in any kind of weather. And just a mile outside this ledge lie the deep waters of the Jeffery Basin. These waters were rich environment for bluefin, with islands and edges serving as fish magnets, attracting vast schools of tuna chow, the perfect place for the bluefin to feed and have a run.

Carl started fishing these new waters year around, setting lobster traps, or throwing harpoons. He soon learned the underwater terrain, where the sea mounts were located-the hard and soft bottoms, the shallow waters, and the deep, where the mackerel, herring, and menhaden would swim.

How did Carl know that these tuna were the same body of fish that he and brother Herbie-and Orlando Wallace and Oscar and Merle Gilliam before them-had been chasing in the waters around Small Point? Easy. They knew the fish, just as the fish knew the boats.

With the arrival of the McIntire's, Perkins Cove turned into the tuna capital of the world. Carl was in his prime as a harpooner bringing in a hundred fish or more every summer on the *Priscilla Cameron*. And he was leading a whole new group of youngsters out to sea to chase the bluefin.

I would be one of them.

Billy Tower and Leon Perkins. Perkins Cove, late 1940-1950 era.

Photo from McIntire Family

11.

Best Years

In the 1950s, harpooning tuna fish became a fine art, as other fishermen from Gloucester, Newbury Port, Cape Cod, all had brought their individual ideas to the fishery. The bonds of friendships grew stronger, and the fishermen were chasing the fish from Cape Cod to the Canadian line. Some of them would look back on those days and say they were the best years ever.

One of them was Jack Cadario, the son of an Italian immigrant, who learned the art of harpooning from Al Kiser, a well-known Massachusetts tuna fisherman. Al would soon watched the young man he just trained up buy his own boat and quickly turn a lot of heads. Cadario, in his open thirty-foot boat named *Hell Diver*, started covering up the town dock in Plum Island, Newburyport, Massachusetts with massive tuna fish. He saved enough money to buy have a thirty-four foot Novi model, built in Canada, which he called the *Diane,* a boat everybody would soon know by sight.

In 1952 and 1953 a bunch of smaller bluefin, two to three hundred pound fish, came into middle banks outside of Gloucester, in bunches numbering in the thousands. On one epic day, the *Diane* rode into one of these massive schools and Jack started putting flags out. Then Jack hauled back a few fish right on to the boat; the small size of the fish made this possible. Then he charged right back into the bunch again. At the end of the day twenty six fish were piled up on the deck of *Diane*, a new record. Jack Cadario had just set the bar very high.

The *Diane,* for the next few years, harpooned more bluefin than pretty much any other boat on the coast. Unfortunately the *Diane* was lost in Hurricane Carol, which pounded New England in August 1954, claiming three thousand boats.

The Army would also claim Jack. Not long after he lost his boat, the poor guy was sent to Germany. Actually, there was nothing poor about him. Jack was a money magnet. When he returned from the service, his good fortune continued. Just about every investment he made-every business venture he got involved in--turned into a smashing success. An avid big game hunter, his home was like a museum. A self-made millionaire by his early thirties, Jack would build some incredible boats. He elevated the art of harpooning bluefin.

For Sonny McIntire all those years of throwing broken rake handles in the backyard finally paid off. In 1955, at fifteen years of age, he ironed his first fish near Boon Island. It wasn't long before everyone in the vicinity knew who this young man was.

Sonny heard of a monster fish seen off York Ledge and on the way out he told his dad. The ledge was not an area where fish usually ran, but it was early in the year and his father agreed to have a look. A couple of other boats were in the area and none of them saw any fish. By late afternoon the McIntire's were the lone boat, and as it sometimes happens, that's when the fish showed up.

They put out a flag on the first bunch they chased. That bunch popped right back up and soon they had a second flag in the water. These two fish didn't go very far before dying, and they hauled them both back to the boat. It was almost dark now. They were packing up the boat for the return trip to the Cove when a triple-three fish swimming together-popped up right in front of their boat.

Carl on the stand said he could barely see the fish that he threw at. Sonny, up in the mast, could see them better. His dad had hit the small one in the bunch. They put out a flag. An hour later that last flag was still towing hard. The fish was still strong and showing no signs of slowing. All they could do was follow the flag end as close as they dared so they would not lose it. It was ten o'clock at night when the fish finally died.

They were now ten miles offshore. When Carl and Sonny finally hauled the fish along side the boat, they found themselves looking at a bluefin was beyond massive. When they lifted the fish onto the boat with the block and tackle, the *Priscilla Cameron* listed under its incredible weight. All Sonny could think was if this was the small fish in that bunch of three, how bloody big were the other two?

When the fish went to Boston, the McIntire's got paid for a thousand pounds **of** tuna, dressed weight, meaning the weight of the fish minus the head, guts, and tail. They put the fish on the largest scale the dealer had, which could handle up to one thousand pounds. The dressed fish bottomed out the scale.

How big was that tuna fish? Sonny estimated it at seventeen hundred to eighteen hundred pounds live weight, which would be a world record. What the McIntire's had managed to do was catch one of the grandest of the Small Point Fish and the largest fish Sonny has ever seen.

Another time when Sonny was in his teens he went out fishing with his mother near Boon Island. They saw a single wake, which Sonny could see was not a bluefin, but a shark about fifteen feet long. Thinking it was a big mako, his mom yelled at him to iron the shark. Sonny threw out at the shark and missed. The shark turned and attacked the boat, slamming into the side with such force, they realized it wasn't a mako, but a great white. His mother thought this was funny as hell.

 When the shark popped back up in the water, his mom lined the boat up and went right back up on it. Still laughing, she encouraged Sonny to have another go at the beast. Sonny, who did not want anything to do with the shark, took the dart off the pike. When his mom drove him on the fish, he gave it a poke with the pole. Well, that just pissed off the shark some more. The shark turned and launched itself up out of the water right under Sonny's feet. The stand in their boat was quite low, only seven or eight feet off the water. Sonny said he could have dropped a bushel basket in the great white's mouth before its jaws snapped shut just inches under his feet.

For good measure, the shark then bit the boat a half a dozen times. The attacks were so violent, Sonny had to go below to make sure they were not taking on water. The whole time his mom was laughing and clapping. She thought it was the funniest thing she ever saw, Sonny didn't think so. He was still shaking from the sight of those open jaws trying to bite his feet off. He looked at his mother a little differently after the shark encounter. The woman had a strange sense of humor.

Priscilla was the ultimate outdoors woman. She loved to deer hunt, tuna fish, and she was the best cook on the planet. She was a Down East woman. Some silly shark snapping his jaws off the side of the boat didn't scare her.

Jack with big bluefin, 1954. Photo from Cadario Family

Knickerbocker, 1940-1950's era.

Tiger Too, 1950-1960's era. Photo's from Holt

Wayne Holt, 1962. Photo from Holt

12.

Big Mother Russian Trawlers

By the later 1950s, the Small Point Fish were hunted in earnest, by not only by small vessels in the feeding grounds, but by huge noisy ships, airplanes, and baited hooks set even in their spawning area. The fish had no peace. They were pursued incessantly. They knew they could not survive these new threats. They could not go back to the summer feeding at Small Point or even Boon Island. These were now killing waters.

Now they stayed far offshore and swam deep as they migrated north from the Gulf of Mexico. They kept right on traveling past the Maine waters, past Boon Island, Jordan Basin, Browns Bank, past the Rips, and other areas where they had once congregated. They swam into much colder water than ever before and still they traveled.

The *Fairtry,* built in 1953, was the very first factory trawler. The *Fairtry* launched what would become the distant water fleet, a group of factory boats from many nations that would industrialize fishing on an unprecedented scale.

I know trawlers. I've spent a good part of my life operating factory trawlers. I even had a small percentage ownership in one. I know a lot about them. They have their place in the world of fishing. They produce some of the best seafood in the world. But like anything that goes unchecked, these rigs can really mop up an area and do a lot of damage to the eco-system that sustains both man and fish.

At the time, the fishing waters of the United States extended only 12 miles offshore. Soon factory trawlers from Russia, Japan, West Germany, Spain and Portugal lit up the waters off Maine like an offshore city. These foreign boats would invade the best fishing areas—the Platts, Three Dory Ridge, and Jeffreys Bank-and pound the bottom till the remaining fish were all broken up in the water column. What had been a school of fish was now a scattering of individual fish mixed with others. Once the cod, haddock, and dabs were caught, the boats would switch out and go after the herring, mackerel, and squid. And those schools would be destroyed too.

The Russian trawlers were known as BMRT's. To us that stood for Big Mother Russian Trawlers, though the initials mean something else in Russian. These boats were about 300 feet long had a crew of a 100 or more, both men and women. They could produce around a 100 metric tons of frozen product a day. And the BMRT's would stay at sea for a couple years or more.

In the 1960's the Soviet Union was a superpower. They had hundreds of thousand of Red Army soldiers and personnel to feed, so they built a lot of BMRT's and sent them to the best fishing areas of the North Atlantic. They traveled as a fleet sharing information. Once they found a body of fish, thirty BMRT's would hammer the area.

The result was devastation. Imagine, a logger and his team are pointed at a cedar forest in the Pacific Northwest, and told have at it. There are the trees. You get paid for every one you cut down. There are no limits or no laws about how many. Those loggers are going to go cut down every tree. That is what these foreign boats did and what our government let them do, even though the Russians were our Cold War enemy. Our fish stocks have yet to rebound from that calamity.

This is what the tuna fishermen of the 1960's encountered: an invasion of monster steel rigs harvesting ground-fish on a massive scale just outside their offshore lobster fishery. As the ecosystem was ravaged, the bluefin went elsewhere. The fish that came every summer to the waters around Small Point and Boon Island in the tens of thousands just disappeared.

It wasn't just the factory trawlers. There were also Japanese long liners, which set down miles of baited surface gear to catch bluefin and swordfish. The Japanese had discovered the spawning grounds of the bluefin in the Gulf of Mexico in the late 1950 and then followed the fish north into the New England waters.

Then there were the purse seiners-some flagged in Canada, others in the United States--targeting the bluefin with their massive nets, which they wrapped around schools of fish and captured them as if in a gigantic purse.

In early 1960's two of the most famous bluefin purse seiners, the U.S.-flagged ships, *Ferrante* and the *Western Star*, came from the West Coast via the Panama Canal and made the waters off New Bedford, Massachusetts their new home port.

This was the dark ages for the bluefin. Up till now the only threat the fish really had was a few guys throwing poles at them in the summers. Not anymore.

Record-keeping about the annual bluefin catch began in the early 1960s. Until then, a handful of harpooners landed whatever fish they caught and records like Jack Cadario's big day were mostly a matter of lore among the fishermen.

Now the big players were fully involved in the fishery. Even with a low price of 10 to 20 cents per pound, the West Coast seiners and the Japanese long liners reported huge catch numbers. More than 3,700 metric tons of bluefin were landed in 1962; the next year it was over 5,400 metric tons. The numbers reported by the Japanese were surely understated but they were staggering as well. Add the Soviet factory trawlers, and we are extremely lucky that the whole ecosystem did not collapse.

NOAA Central Library Historical Fisheries Collection.
A standard Mayakovskiy 278 foot stern trawler. The back bone of the Soviet fishing fleet. With a crew of 100 they could stay at sea for 3 months at a time.

The harpooners adapted as best they could. They searched up and down the coast. They chased the migrating fish farther offshore. They built new boats, like Ed Gerry's *Scoot.*

I was a boy and excited to be riding boats watching Carl McIntire haul fish. I was too young to know those were actually dark years in the fishery. Many young men who might have been fishermen were knee deep in the rice paddies of Vietnam throwing grenades instead of harpoons. Our fish stocks were being raped by the factory ships. The Small Point Fish had all but disappeared. It wasn't until 1977 that the United States Congress finally acted.

The hey days. Photo from Brazier

13.

The 70's

In April 1976, Congress passed the Magnuson-Stevens Fishery Conservation and Management Act. The law, signed by President Gerald Ford, established a two hundred mile fishing limit as of January 1977. It is tempting to say "better late than never," but that would be premature. Years of uncontrolled fishing by the foreign factory trawler fleets had devastating effects on our fish stocks. It has been forty years since the two hundred mile limit went into effect and the ground-fish have still not rebounded.

The fishermen of New England were set back a hundred years. Fish stocks were so depleted that fishermen had to change fisheries, move to Alaska, or get out of the business altogether. Families that fished for generations lost their boats.

One of the few good things that would come out of this environmental disaster was a new market for bluefin tuna fishermen. With the two hundred mile limit now in effect, the Japanese could no longer set hundreds of miles of baited long line hooks off Georges Bank. They now had to buy bluefin from U.S. fishermen. Overnight, the bluefin was worth real money. The sport of harpooning became a business and the fishery was launched in whole new direction.

It wasn't always pretty. To protect the fishery the National Marine Fisheries Service (NMFS) started passin g new regulations and laws, some of which made no sense. Starting in 1977, tuna fishermen would be allowed one fish a day. This went over like an un-baited hook. Every tuna fisherman from New York to Maine was ready to storm Capitol Hill. So the feds stopped and listened to the fishermen. Dana Kangas, a Gloucester harpooner, had a direct hand in coming up with a tagging program. The idea was to tag fish, so that the NMFS could learn about migration patterns and better protect the stock. Kangas proposed that, for every five fish that a boat tagged the boat would get a chit for an extra fish, which could be used after August 20th, when the one-a-day limit was changed so that all seven fish could be caught on one day. The boats could increase their catch by applying the chits they earned from tagging. They threw us a carrot.

The concept of tagging was brand new in 1977 and it did not go well. The first tags distributed by NMFS were tuna darts with long brightly colored streamers. The harpooners would just use their regular harpoons with the new tags. But the twenty four inch long pikes, designed to drive the dart deep into the body of the fish, often killed the fish that was supposed to be tagged. When Carl McIntire killed the very first fish he tried to tag, he went below and threw all the tags overboard. Fishermen were also tagging sharks, sunfish, even pilot whales, and claiming them as tagged bluefin. I remember seeing one ocean sunfish in Cape Cod Bay that had so many colored tags it looked like a Christmas tree.

But the program did start to work. The big darts were switched out for small plastic tags. The fishermen cut the size of their pikes from twenty four inches to three or four inches in length. This minimized hitting the fish in the spine or burying the tag too deep. The feds clamped down on tagging other creatures, and bluefin were successfully tagged.

On the flip side, the regulations brought the dark side of commercial fishing out to front and center. So many laws were broken it bordered on ridiculous. I remember coming into Perkins Cove with two fish. To evade the feds, we were going to tie off the extra fish to the bell buoy a mile off shore, and come back to pick it up after midnight. A lot of other fishermen had the same plan. When we returned there were seven or eight fish tied off to the bell buoy, which was half sunk from their weight. The feds could not keep up with every new angle the fishermen could dream up, and the whole program was scrapped after two years.

The same kinds of challenges face the NMFS today. Are they managing the fishery? Or the fishermen?

This all happened in my youth. I saw first hand my peers breaking law after stupid law. I learned the government was not the friend of the commercial fishermen, and breaking laws was just normal behavior. I learned the feds and fisherman was a game, and we all played to win. It was a lesson that would come back to haunt me later in life. When the other side wins, it is life changing.

Jack on *Susan C*, 1970. Photo from Cadario Family

I told the story in my first book, *A Hard Way To Make An Easy Living*. In Alaska I was caught breaking the law in a way that was common at the time, and it was no game. My actions cost me everything I owned: homes, ownership in ship, and my marriage. I lost a way of life, along with millions of dollars in assets and potential earning income.

Older and (I hope) wiser, what I want to pass on to commercial fishermen is this: we make our living by what we put in the hole, be it a harpooned bluefin or three hundred metric tons of codfish. We need a set of rules. Look at what happened in the era of the rapacious factory trawlers. We need an NMFS to look out for the fishing stock. We also need the American Bluefin Tuna Association to look out for the fisherman, to make sure the ocean is, as they say, a level playing field.

Al Kiser, hand line. Ipswich Bay, 1971. Photo from Holt

Eric Brazier with Kermit and Mike Horning, 1978-1980 era. Photo from Brazier

Corky wins Bailey Island Bluefin
Tournament with George Wyman.
First place cup for 615 lb bluefin
in 1982
Photos from Wyman

Dana Kangas throws and hits a 900 lb single running bluefin from his boat the Coot, 1970's era. Photos from Kangas

Corky with bluefin catch, 1970's era. Photo from Wyman

Susie E, 1970's era. Photo from Edgley

14.

Unification Church

By the late 1970s, the harpoon fishery evolved in ways Orlando Wallace never could have imagined. After two years of lobbying NMFS to change the one-a-day limit, the tuna fishermen got their wish. The government established a system of quotas for three different types of boats that remains in effect to this day.

In the harpoon category, boats were allowed to catch multiple fish per day, but could only harvest the fish by harpoon.

In the general category, the boats were still limited to one a day, but they had the choice to take their fish by either hook or harpoon.

In the seine category, all of the working boats were grandfathered in; no new boats could come into the fishery.

Each group was given an annual tonnage allotment. Once the boats in that category had caught their allotment, they were done for the year.

In 1979 there were twenty nine harpoon boats, which were allowed to bring sixty metric tons of fish. That was a hefty quota, even split twenty nine ways. For that season, at least bank accounts were fattened up.

With the new Japanese market came quality control, something the tuna fisherman of early days didn't know much about. They would boat a fish and maybe have a tarp thrown over it. The fish would lay on deck in the sun all day and maybe get headed and gutted, or maybe not.

The Japanese sent over quality inspectors who graded the fish right on the dock. The fish that were bled, had good fat content and were in top condition got the highest price tag. The fishermen responded quickly to satisfy the demands of the buyers

As more boats joined the harpoon category in the next year few years, the quota was caught by mid-season. The hard-core harpoon guys, led by Carl McIntire, either purchased or leased a second boat to fish the general category. With the price of fish going up, the fishery was now becoming more popular. With more boats and the quotas remaining the same, the pie was now being divided up into smaller slices.

The fishermen created networks to compete, which bred tension. In years past everyone pretty much shared information. The Ogunquit boats would talk with the Gloucester guys on open CB or VHF channels. Everyone knew what the other guys were doing and catching. Not anymore. Radio scramblers were the norm, and boats left out of the network resented it. With the money came greed or competition or some combination of the two.

The original twenty nine harpoon boats formed the Tri-Coastal Cooperative to develop the bluefin market and educate the fishermen about handling techniques to get the best price possible. The cooperative distributed red tee-shirts with a picture of a bluefin on the back with the slogan, 'Eat it Raw' in big letters. They were like a bikers club colors, and wearing them became was a very cool thing.

As the boats learned how to properly care for the bluefin, prices rose and suddenly it seemed like everyone was a tuna fisherman. With the new money, came new interest groups and organizations, most notably the Unification Church, whose members were often referred to as the Moonies by local fishermen and general public.

Around 1980 the Reverend Sun Myung Moon of South Korea bought a waterfront building in Gloucester, Massachusetts. The new owners were a bit different from the traditional Italian fish brokers of the area. South Korea is a country whose level of devotion to a fish diet is exceeded only by the Japanese. Rev. Moon had a passion for fishing, all types of fishing, he once designed a fishing boat for himself and had a vision for the bluefin tuna industry involving improving the livelihood of fisherman as reflected in many of his speeches. So his church began buying and processing bluefin tuna.

At first, the church tried to buy from anyone, offering a little more money per pound. Their perceived cult status made locals very uncomfortable, to put it mildly. Rev. Moon was thought to style himself as a messiah on par with Jesus and his church looked very much like a cult to locals. Few fishermen would sell them the fish they so desperately wanted. Rev. Moon solved that problem by turning his followers into fishermen. If no one would sell them tuna, they would just go out and catch their own

Now, you cannot just learn to be a harpooner overnight but you can catch bluefin by hook and line, and this requires less skill. Throw enough baited hooks in the water, and sooner or later, the bait will be eaten.

A fleet of little white open boats, manned by the faithful, appeared on the Middle Bank off of Gloucester. They didn't catch a lot at first but as more boats were added, more fish came into their processing plant. Soon their successful enterprise was dug in deep as a tick on a hound dog in one of New England's oldest fishing communities.

To be honest no one knew what, if anything, to do about it. The Japanese market was so new and the fishery was changing so fast, that the arrival of Unification Church just added a new level of weirdness to it all.

The hand line fleet-the boats catching tuna with hooks-turned into this massive floating city on the Middle Banks. There were two hundred boats, including just about every type of vessel that could be put to sea: open fiberglass outboards, lobster boats, and sport fishing boats. There were even buy boats, which would purchase the tuna right there on the water.

It was crazy. With this much chum in the water, the tuna were sucked into the area every day, resulting in some really big catch days. The harpoon boats also took advantage of this new fleet of "hookers," as these new boats were dubbed. The bluefin would feed in the chum slick in the mornings, and then be found running on the surface outside of the fleet in the afternoons. The harpoon boats were waiting for them.

When the church fleet peaked in numbers, it seemed like there were a hundred of their white boats on the water every day. The other rod and reel boats might have had a different opinion, but the harpoon fisherman pretty much left them alone. They were doing their own thing and not harming anyone. They might have even done some good, not that anyone would say that back then, but of course hind sight is clearer. They were another tuna exporter. They always kept their offered price high-usually fifty cents or more a pound above the base price set by Tri-Coastal Cooperative. They did their thing and we did ours.

Unification Church fishing fleet, 1980's era.

Photo courtesy of Family Federation for World Peace and Unification

(Former Unification Church)

15.

Billie Mac

In the late 1970's Sonny McIntire owned a large Eastern rig dragger called the *Vandal,* which he used to catch fish by towing a net over the side. In the midst of a big nor'easter the *Vandal* went up on a piling during the storm which drove a massive hole though her. She sank at the dock. Back then insurance wasn't always carried, especially on wooden draggers, and Sonny lost just about everything.

That winter Sonny and his two sons Billy and his older brother Bobby, went to work helping their dad rebuild the *Streaker* as a glass over wood boat for lobstering and harpooning. Those were the same brothers I had first laid eyes on when I was five years old. Since then Billy Mac had become my best friend. We started fishing on his dad's boat when were kids in the 1960s. We grew up together in the 1970's. We were the cove rats, the wild ones, the generation that fished hard and stayed up late. We lived and breathed bluefin.

Billy was the best of us. He grew up on the decks of Sonny's boats and together they took the rest of us to school when it came to harpooning time. As good as old Carl and Sonny were in the 1950's and 1960's, Sonny and Billy of the 1970's to 2000's were even better.

They went to building the *Streaker* into a whole new rig: old wooden lobster boat with a fiberglass hull, a huge V-8 Oldsmobile engine in her bilge and a stand and tower to see the fish. It was a hard long winter for the family, but they pushed though, and by the time spring arrived the boat, now re-christened the *Streaker* was on her mooring in the Cove.

For the next six or seven years the McIntire's fished that old boat hard, both lobstering and catching bluefin tuna. They used back yard engineering and what was on hand, rigging up rope controls and steering in the tuna tower that probably only Billy and his dad could even operate, let alone excel with. While the rest of the tuna fleet was all switching over to high-end, high-dollar fiberglass hulls, the McIntire's sailed this homely, homemade craft with a pulpit pointed up off the bow at a steep angle. When Sonny was in the stand, it looked like his head was at Billy's feet level in the mast. At any distance, the old gray boat blended into the horizon so well that you only saw two men suspended above the water, like magic. For years, the two of them caught more bluefin than the rest of us combined.

Billy was a free spirit; he lived for the now. The future would take care of itself. He would literally give you his last dollar out of his pocket; forgo a meal himself if you were hungry, or jump overboard and to save a drowning girl. Billy lived and breathed bluefin. For him there were two times of year, two seasons, when the fish were here and when they weren't. Billy made his nest egg every summer. The winter money would never last the winter no matter how big the egg was. It was all about today, every day of Billy Mac's life.

In 1980 Sonny and Billy made history. The first day out that year they caught seven fish, and never looked back. That summer Billy and his dad would catch more than sixty tuna fish. A boat would have a good day and be offloading four fish at the bait dock, then under the old footbridge in would steam the old *Streaker* listing over, near sunk and freighted to the rails with tuna fish.

This was the summer after Billy and I graduated from high school. Did we ever sleep? I remember Billy and I walking down to the Cove at sun up one morning. Neither one of us had been to bed, it was going to be a harpoon day. Billy and his dad already had fifty something fish, where old Bucko and I had five. I told Billy I hoped I could stay awake in the mast today. Billy stopped in his tracks and just looked at me. "That is why you only have five fish," is all he said. He kept on walking with me down to the boats. I never forgot that. For Billy, no matter what he lived though the night before, harpooning was what was the most important thing in the morning. It was a wonderful way to grow up. We had so much freedom. My parents knew I was tuna fishing and they might not see me for a month. No cell phones, no internet. We were on the Cape one week, Down East the next. Every year the last week of July, was the Bailey Island Tuna Tournament, held at Mackerel Cove Marina; boats from all over New England would arrive for a week of heavy fishing and crazy partying.

The tournament had a harpoon category and it was always one of the weeks we would circle every summer.

The owner of marina was named Bill. Billy and I hounded this guy endlessly for a couple of the marina's shirts. They were red golf shirts with a bluefin on the front pocket and Mack Cove Marina printed on the logo. We wanted a couple. Finally the guy told us we had to either work at the marina or sleep with someone who did to get a shirt.

Billy just looked at me and said, "I hope you can fit into a small."

He did what he had to do. The next morning at breakfast Billy and I were both wearing those tight red tee shirts.

After I moved away, I didn't see Billy as often but he didn't change. In his fifties he was the very same person he was in his twenties. He didn't want anything out of life besides his family, his friends and his tuna fish. He did not want the responsibility that came along with raising a family or owning a bunch of stuff. He made his money each year, and he spent it. The next year would come and he would do it all again.

Billy Mac died on a full moon night in August 2013. He and a few friends untied his boat, the *Clover*, and went out for a midnight cruise from Perkins Cove. A mile offshore one of the girls decided to go for a swim. She jumped overboard and got caught in the current. Billy went in after her. After a very long time, an exhausted Billy got the girl back to the boat. He saved her life and in doing so gave his. If you could have asked Billy Mac if he could choose which way he would meet his maker, that's probably the way he would have wanted it.

When I learned that Billy was missing and how it happened, it did not surprise me, I spent a sleepless night, remembering so many incredible times with Billy: Drinking endless rum and Cokes in Bailey Island. Walking though the dark streets of Provincetown looking for women to take us home and let us shower. We lived like nomads as harpooners; showers were always our best pick up line.

I thought about the old timer in Alaska who told me that fishermen who die at sea come back as sea birds. I remember grabbing his arm and asking, "I'm coming back as a frigging seagull?"

He laughed and told me no. More likely an albatross.

Well, Billy Mac I still talk to you a lot. When I'm tuna fishing, which is pretty. much all the time, I never harm a seagull in my life. When they come around my boat, I have no clue which one is you. So I feed every damn bird that comes near me.

Billy Mac with Jordan, his niece, not long before he passed.

Photo from McIntire Family.

16.

Year of the Prong

In June 1982 Eric Brazier, a lobsterman out of Perkins Cove, took the first harpoon fish of the season on Jeffreys Bank, a piece of bottom otherwise known the Prong. The Prong is not very large, just a few square nautical miles in size, which covers an undersea ledge of the kind that attracts fish.

In 1982 there was something about this little area that the bluefin liked because a mass of fish arrived in June of that year and never left till September. They were huge: seven hundred to nine hundred pounds dressed was the norm. It did not take long for boats from as far as upstate Maine to Cape Cod to converge on the Prong. Now a few square miles of ocean might be pretty spacious if you are paddling a kayak, but if not if you are manning a harpoon boat. With the arrival of fifty or more boats, it sometimes felt like we were fishing in a bathtub.

Small bunches of fish-anywhere from three to a dozen would pop up and run for a short burst amongst all the boats. Two or three boats would see the same bunch and go for them at the same time. Tempers were short and a lot of arguments were hashed out from the towers of different boats.

Jack Cadario was late to arrive that year, coming to the Prong half-way through the season. He had been doing what wooden boat owners did if they had a rig like Jackie's *Cobra,* a 48-foot Royal Lowell. He had been remodeling. His first day on the Prong, he ironed four fish. I had four fish for the whole year, and he boated as many in his first day out.

That hurt like hell. My shipmate, Captain Brian "Bucko" Burke, was just about have a heart attack in the mast beside me, I kept asking him what the bloody hell is Jack's boat chasing? This really set Bucko off because he couldn't tell. The fish were not leaving a wake. They were swimming ten feet underwater, and Jack was still seeing them.

The *Cobra* helped him for sure. It was a special boat. Built for harpooning, she had a forty-foot mast mounted behind the twenty-foot tower. I remember seeing it for the first time and thinking Jackie had brass balls going up that thing. Rick Thurlow was Jack's full-time mate, a graduate of Maine Maritime, the school for anyone joining for the Merchant Marine. Ricky was always working at something on the *Cobra*. I never forgot that: someone taking so much pride in something they truly loved. You stepped on board the *Cobra,* you were in a whole different league. It was like everybody else was playing college football, and Jack Cadario was the NFL.

Every time I saw his boat, I visited him. He told me stores about hunting in Africa and Alaska. He was an amazing person: Zane Grey, Ernest Hemingway, and Wilbur Smith, all wrapped up in a harpooner. And though he was among the best in the world, he would still let the young guys throw.

When I was just starting out as a kid in the early 1970s, he gave me my first opportunities to throw at a fish. With everyone else I would beg them all summer long to have one throw. With Jackie, I never even had to even ask.

"Corky," he'd say, "You're up."

God I loved that man.

Bucko was a very different harpooner but just as unique. Jack was a millionaire; Bucko was a nomad. Jack's house looked like a museum. Bucko would go two weeks without a shower.

A great chef, Bucko loved to cook. He would prepare meals for ten boats at ten o'clock at night. After off-loading their fish, the fishermen would raft up for a meal from Bucko. He would hand them plate of home-made stew and offer a spoon he had just wiped off on a dirty shirt he had been wearing for a week.

One day that summer we were steaming for the Prong on a flat calm July morning, taking the four-hour jog at seven knots. When we finally arrived at the Prong, guys are already out in stands and flag ends are getting towed everywhere.

A single bluefin pops up-huge, massive, grand. The fish is plowing in a straight line. Bucko is out on the stand. I see the fish disappear over Bucko's right shoulder, and...he doesn't throw. The damn fish hit the bow of the boat. The beast reappeared from under Bucko's feet.

"Bucko?" I screamed. "Why didn't you throw?"

Bucko just made his way out of the stand across the roof and painfully climbed back into the mast, not saying a word. I slid over so he could have the steering station.

"Bucko?"

"I just forgot to throw," is all he said.

"No one forgets to throw at a barn door," I screamed.

Bucko just hung his head. He had just froze up.

The harpooners stayed with the Prong fish all summer. No one really knew or cared if they were missing other opportunities elsewhere. When the last single was chased and the fish finally migrated back south in September, that magical season was over.

No one had huge numbers but the catch was spread out pretty evenly through the whole fleet. The highline boats, led by Jack Cadario, had twenty or so fish for the whole summer, not a lot by comparison with other years. At the same time, everyone had a dozen or so. The fish were big fat beasts that brought top dollar at the auction houses in Tokyo. No one got rich in 1982 but no one had to sell their boats either.

This was the last year in which I remember everyone working together. Carl and Sonny McIntire were there and they were catching most of the fish. Along side of them were everybody else: Linc and his dad Riley, from New Hampshire, tied up next to the 'Down Easters', Bradley and Kevin on the *Poor Boy*; to Eric Brazier rafted outside of the *Cobra.* Everyone got along. Everyone seemed to share information. We lived on five gallon buckets of rum and Cokes. It was crowded sometimes but we were all in the same ball game.

Two years later, restless and hungry to see the world, I moved to Alaska. My sister had moved there and had a friend making sixty thousand dollars a years. I thought I would just go to make enough money to buy a harpoon boat and come back in a year. I didn't return for twenty years.

Jackie and Ricky Thurlow unloading swordfish, Kennebunkport.

Photo from Cadario family

Eric Brazier. Photo from Brazier

Poor Boy. Photo from Simmones

BOOK III
TOMORROW

17.

Nova Scotia

For years I had been hearing about the bluefin which ran in the waters off Prince Edward Island and northern Nova Scotia. I watched the video and I read the articles, but some things you just need to see by yourself. So in September 2014, I made a trip to Ballantynes Cove, nestled next to the town of Antigonish in Nova Scotia, with a couple of buddies to try something that was never done before: catch a Canadian giant bluefin on a hand-held spinning rod. We did it but that was not the highlight of the trip.

What I saw in Nova Scotia was beyond anything I have ever experienced in my lifetime. Now I know how Orlando Wallace felt when he first took his harpoon in hand. We were fishing just a few miles outside the breakwater in a hundred feet of water and we chummed hundreds of monster tuna to the surface. In size they ranged from five hundred to well over a thousand pounds-and we hand-fed them.

One of my buddies was on Fisherman's Bank, a ledge twenty miles away. Another was fishing on Prince Edward Island forty miles away. We all experienced the exact same thing. There were tens of thousands, if not hundreds of thousands, of giant bluefin tuna in the waters of northern Canada. I had found the Small Point Fish! I did not believe it was possible. The bluefin were tame, as if they knew we were of no threat to them.

The reason? In Canada, fishermen are only allowed to harvest one fish per season. The rules state that once a fish is hooked the angler is only allowed one hour to leader the fish along side. If the battle goes beyond an hour the fish must be cut free, and you must also use barbless offset circle hooks, nothing else is legal. It is the perfect system for a sport-fishery.

Bluefin are extremely intelligent creatures, as smart as dolphins, I believe. The brain of a thousand pound fish would require two hands to hold it. The fish have learned and adapted. In fact they come to the boats to get fed. There is no way they would act like this if the Canadians were killing them as we do in U.S. waters. After seeing these fish myself I was convinced that they came from the same gene pool as the fish from Small Point, and by God I was going to prove it.

Nova Scotia, Canada 2014, hand feeding giant bluefin on *Rough Rider.*

Photo from Decker

My wife Maggie knows me better than I know myself. As soon as she met me at the Tampa airport after my trip to Canada in the fall of 2014, and I started talking, she just knew. She had that "here we go again" look. She held my hand and heard me out on the way to baggage claim, as I hashed out what I wanted to do. I knew that these tuna were not getting by the Maine harpoon boats. They were not swimming up the New England coast. The fish now harvested in the U.S. harpoon fishery do not come from the same school as the giants I saw in Canada.

But, if that's true, where do the Canadian bluefin come from? They come to Canada every August, feed for a couple of months and then go off to spawn. Where? I have no idea. But I want to know.

As soon as I returned from Canada I called Adrian Gray and Jack Vitek, two friends who are active in the International Game Fish Association. I convinced them they should come to Antigonish, and they did. Adrian and Jack spent a couple wonderful days on the *Rough Rider*, catching and filming fish. The result was a beautiful article in the 2015 IGFA World Record Yearbook.

Canada is our laboratory, our opportunity to really learn about this body of fish. The technology is available, and the Canadian fishery is the perfect test bed. The same has been done for sharks, where a lot of money has been spent tagging great whites off Chatham on Cape Cod. The Discovery Channel has a Shark Week. Why not a Bluefin Week? Ideally, we would put some long-range satellite tracking on these fish to learn where they go to spawn. Wherever that place is, it should be protected.

To test my theory about the origins of these fish, I needed a boat, one that could venture far offshore. I knew where to look. Back in the 1990's the U.S. harpooners caught the annual quota pretty early every year. Many had two boats: one in the harpoon and a second in the general. When daily limit in the general category was increased from one a day to three or four a day, most of the guys sold off their second boats.

But David Lenny, an old-time harpooner from York, Maine decided not to sell. He had put a lot of money into his second boat, an Ellis purchased in 2000, so he just stored it in his barn. In January 2015 David, now age seventy five, agreed to sell it to me.

The boat was in good shape. In storage for eleven years, she had only been used for a couple of summers and had less than thousand hours on the engine. Over the years David had cannibalized some of the gear, namely the harpoon stand, the tower, and the electronics. So I had to rig the boat from scratch, using every penny I could get my hands on. I did not care. I had to have her.

Four months after my trip to Nova Scotia, I drove from Florida to Maine. I arrived in York in mid April, pulling an overloaded U-Haul with my hunting truck. I spent the next six weeks, working twelve hours a day turning that boat into the harpoon boat that I christened the *Maggie.*

Maggie coming out of her cocoon and refurbished, 2015. Photo's from Decker.

18.

Boothbay

My harpoon partner these days is a sixty three year old boat builder from Boothbay, Maine named Bradley Simmones. He builds one boat a year for selected clients. He also tends hundreds of moorings in Boothbay. I've known Bradley my whole life, and always admired his expertise and his personal style.

I first met Bradley in the late 1970's. He owned a boat that looked very much like Sonny McIntire's *Streaker:* a wooden lobster boat, with a big ass gas engine, a pulpit that pointed to the moon, it was called the *Poor Boy.* Bradley also had Kevin Wilson fishing with him. Kevin was one of the best mates in the fishery.

I remember Bradley came into Perkins Cove one night to offload a couple of fish, after a big day on Jeffreys Bank. Pretty soon the bait dock was covered up in tuna fish. There was a big party that night with lots of beer drunk and fish stories told till well after midnight.

The next morning the harbormaster, Bud Perkins, was cursing all of us. There were harpoon boats on every dock and two or three boats together on the moorings. There were a lot of bloody tuna heads lying about. Everyone was hungover and barely awake, except Bud who was livid and letting us know in profane detail about the full measure of worthlessness as human beings. What I remember most about meeting Bradley for the first time was how cool he was handling that pissed off old man.

While I was in Alaska, he was on the water every summer. Bradley has harpooned hundreds of fish in his lifetime but he sold his harpoon boat in 2014 and planned to retire from fishing. There was no way in hell I was going to let that happen. I was coming back into the fishery in my fifties and I wanted him on my boat. He finally agreed.

On the *Maggie* we take turns on the pulpit. The rule is, you throw till you miss. That way the guy with the hot hand is on the stand but we both get to throw. Bradley is always up first and since he does not miss much, I'm the back-up quarterback. What makes us a good team is that we know we can both spot fish really well, not an easy task.

We moor the boat in Boothbay, because that is where Bradley's home is. I live in Florida most of the year, so during the harpoon season I camp on the boat. Boothbay is a great place to spend summers. The deep water harbor is protected and the currents and tides are small for a Maine port. While Boothbay is a full-blown tourist mecca in the summer, few places have all the services for fishermen that the town offers. I always loved Boothbay. The bars and women were (and still are) legendary. Except these days I don't drink, I'm married and I'm in bed by eight o'clock.

Nonetheless, camping on the *Maggie* brings back all those memories of youth. The boat is far from a finished. While we have a shower, bunks, and cooking facilities, we don't have a generator. Everything run on twelve volts or it doesn't run at all. There is no air conditioning or heat. The clothes get washed in a bucket. The water is heated by the engine. If we're tied up at the dock, you are going to take a cold shower. The accommodations are primitive by today's standards but still way more comfortable than the boats of my youth when we slept in hammocks, no had showers, and ate our food cold from a cooler. Back then I didn't care. I do now!

My theory about how the Small Point Fish have wound up in Canada is this: If they still breed in the Gulf of Mexico, they must follow the Gulf Stream north, staying way offshore on their route north. This is the only way such a massive body of large fish could have eluded the New England harpoon boats. So maybe they are traveling across the Georges Bank over to Browns Bank on the Canadian side and up the east coast of Nova Scotia. For us to have a crack at them from the U.S. side, we need to find them where they are traveling, which is far, far offshore.

We never did find them in 2015. Bradley and I caught some fish but we never found the mother lode. With one boat and no plane, it was a daunting task. We could have been within a mile of them and never seen them.

The tagging program instituted in Canada in 2015 could help. If we could manage to harpoon a tagged fish in the future, we would learn a lot about these fish. But that's a long shot. The only way to know the migration of the bluefin with certainty would be to have tags that can be read by satellite. Like I say, this has been done with the tagging of the Cape Cod great whites. It could done with the bluefin.

Meanwhile, I'm considering other theories. What if the bluefin no longer spawn in the Gulf of Mexico? What if they are spawning somewhere off the islands of Bermuda? Some huge giants have been caught there in the winter months. If so their route north would be even farther off shore, on the backside of the Georges Bank, not the near shore edge.

Out of reach for the harpooners? No, I'd just need another bladder tank, a generator and an ice machine to get out there.

Maggie at her Boothbay dock. Photo from Decker.

Bradly Simmones with first fish caught on *Maggie*, 2015

Maggie's fish camo bottom painted by Corky. Very sneaky. Photo's from Decker

19.

Markets

When the Tri-Coastal Co-Op was originally formed in the late 1970s, the fish buyers, the middlemen, directed the markets. It is a story as old as fishing itself. If the guy who catches the fish does not sell it direct to the person who eats it, there will be a third party who connects supply with demand and banks most of the money. After the two hundred mile limit went into effect in 1976, the Japanese knew that they would have to deal with the New England fisherman and the buyers of Boston and New York, to get the bluefin they very much wanted to have.

The Japanese also wanted to train the U.S. fishermen about quality, and the easiest way to do that was pay more for a quality fish. When we first start exporting fish, we did not know beans about taking care of a fish to the standards of the Japanese. We would put the fish on deck, bleed it (or not), throw a tarp over it, and continue on. We might head and gut the fish on the way back to shore or we might say "screw it," and crack another beer. Before 1976, the tuna harpooner did not know much about the fish or quality control and never got paid very much.

The Japanese market changed that overnight. The Japanese sent their techs over to New England to grade the fish right on the dock. The would take core samples and temperatures and price the fish accordingly. For one bluefin they might offer a dollar or one dollar fifty cents a pound. For the fish right next to it, they would pay fifty cents a pound. It didn't take long for us to figure out we needed to pack some ice and to clean our fish.

The tuna fishermen like Dana Kangas, Sonny McIntire, Bucko Burke, Eric Brazier, and Jack Cadario formed Tri-Coastal Co-Op, so that they, the fishermen, would direct the bluefin market. It was not easy. Dave Fryburg, a smart businessman, was hired to manage the project. Dave understood the fish buying business, but this was the first time any of us ever dealt with the Japanese. It was a learning process that eventually began to work. The price of the bluefin went up and our relationship with the Japanese buyers improved through the 1980s and early 1990s.

These were the golden years of the fishery Before I left Maine for the Alaska fishery, the most I ever got paid for a bluefin was $5.50 a pound. Less than ten years later Sonny McIntire averaged 18 dollars a pound for an entire one year. Bradley Simmons once got 43 bucks a pound. Pilots were used. Fish were caught. Quotas were filled. New boats were purchased. Harpooners made real money for the first time ever.

It didn't last. As the old timers started to retire or pass on, the core group wasn't replaced with new blood. I had moved to Alaska, for example. Then the Co-Op entered the New England ground-fish market. When the groundfish industry collapsed in the late 1990s, the Co-Op collapsed too.

Buyers from different fisheries moved into fill the void. Now we are back to where we were before the Tri Coastal Co-op. The buyers, not the fishermen, control the domestic and foreign markets. We sell to the buyer we trust the most. It can be a tough business, as I learned in the summer of 2016.

Gary Carter, a buddy from Florida, and I had two successful trips to Georges Banks, landing three on the first voyage and a pair on the second. On trip number three in late September we pulled in three nice fat Canada bluefin. We steamed home one hundred fifty nautical miles, tired but happy, knowing that we would be shipping twelve hundred pounds of quality fat fish to Japan.

All I needed was a buyer. There are four or five major tuna buyers in New England, as well as a couple smaller outfits. One of my harpooning friends had been hounding me for two years to try his buyer, so I finally agreed. I had a good spread of fish, so I called Maggie and told her to arrange pick up with the new buyer. I also had a local option. My harpoon partner Bradley also has a buyer license and we tag and sell a few fish local each summer. I could have sold one of the larger fish to this local market for ten bucks a pound. When I dressed the smallest fish, I noticed its oil was exceptional and would bring the best price over in Japan.

When the pick-up driver for the new buyer arrived, we spoke about this, and he agreed to take the three fish back to his shop, put them in brine, and judge their quality. That was the last I heard from him. The three fish were shipped to Japan. For the first fish, weighing 405 pounds, we received $1,651, about four dollars a pound. The second fish, weighing 478 pounds, brought in $846, less than two dollars a pound. As for the third fish, 90 inches long and weighing 316 pounds, we received nothing. We spent three weeks to get someone from that company to engage in a conversation to see what happened, and still didn't get an answer.

If we had sold that fish, via Bradley, to a sushi restaurant in Boothbay we could have gotten ten bucks a pound. Instead I took a chance with the new buyer-and left about $3,000 on the table.

It was pretty shocking. Now maybe the fish had some ice burn or wasn't up to standard. But why would a professional buyer ship a poor quality fish to the Japanese market with all its associated freight charges and commissions and offer no explanation? We never found out. So I went back to our original buyer. For the last two tuna we caught, he paid $6.50 and $7.00 per pound.

The tuna fisherman gets squeezed from all sides. The commercial wharf in Boothbay, Maine, where I operate in the summer, is the most expensive place to unload a tuna fish on the whole East Coast. The owner charges 50 cents a pound, and the guy who puts the tag in the fish for the buyer charges $75 a fish. For the three fish I landed, it would have cost $850: fifty cents a pound for 1,250 pounds of fish and $75 a fish to the handler.

Needless to say I have made arrangements to take my fish off elsewhere, where I can offload for free or a small dock fee. With its high prices, Boothbay is losing a lot of money in the long run. Tuna fishermen buy a lot of fuel, and harpooners buy even more so. My boat alone spends more than fifteen thousand dollars a season in Boothbay. But if we have to pay exorbitant fees to offload, the harpooners will go elsewhere. We always have.

What a bluefin is worth is determined from the moment the fish is caught. A fish killed by an electric shock harpoon is quickly boated and bled. The head and guts are removed, and the fish is put on ice. Delivered to the dock that night, that fish is the most valuable bluefin caught in the world.

The rod and reel captains up in Nova Scotia have their own trick. They don't harpoon the fish. They catch a fish and tire it out so that they can handle it along side the boat. They then place a line though the fish's gill plate and let the fish swim fish alongside the boat, sometimes for miles. This gives the fish time to cool down. The fish is then killed by lancing it in the gills, where it bleeds out very quickly.

Once the fish leaves the boat, another set of factors determines value. The truck driver who takes the fish to market, if he is good at his job, will take a core sample, and a tail cut. The flesh should have a nice red color, with lots of fat deposits. Core temperatures give you a pretty good idea on quality right on the spot.

Trust is key. I sell my fish to North Atlantic Traders for one reason: Steve "The Gut" Merel. I have known Steve since I was a kid. I sold fish to him when I was teenager. So I trust him. Most of the time when I have sold to someone else, I have a negative experience and I lost money. Lesson learned.

A good tuna buyer will have many markets in the domestic side and a firm, good relationship with the Japanese on the foreign side. A best quality fish, so-called "one grade," will either be sold to an elite domestic client, or sent to Japan. The poorer, lean, burnt, damaged fish (number two or three grade) should be marketed on the domestic side. The Japanese will not pay good money for poor quality fish: it is as simple as that.

Flooded markets are very real, regular occurrence. When the tuna fishermen me have a big kill day, seventy or eighty fish might be shipped overseas in a twenty-four hour period. As a result prices fall. A good day on the Georges Bank can turn into bad day on the dock and there's nothing you can do about it. That's the harpooner's life.

North Atlantic Traders (our fish buyers), Steve (Gut) picking up fish from *Maggie*.
Photo from Decker.

North Atlantic Traders,
Steve (Gut) sampling
and examining fat
content.
Photos from Decker.

Japanese typical fish market auction.

Finished product, bluefin sashimi and sushi. Photo from Decker

20.

Politics

At one time or another I have fished around much of the world and nowhere in my travels have I witnessed the intensity of passion that comes with bluefin fishing. I thought marlin captains were a competitive bunch. They are gentlemen, compared to harpooners.

A bluefin can be sold for top money at auction in Japan bringing a fisherman thousands of dollars back to the boat. With money comes greed, resentment and conflict. A few guys I grew up with, fished on the same boats with thirty or forty years ago, are openly hostile. Why? Only reason I can think of is they see me as a threat. Not really sure why they do, but no one wants to talk about it.

Because the bluefin tuna is the most commercially valuable fish swimming in our oceans, it is not surprising that a wide variety of special interest groups have emerged with very different views on how the fishery should be managed. There is the International Game Fish Association, the American Bluefin Tuna Association, the charter boat groups, the game clubs, and the environmentalists, all clashing over what issues should take precedence. Unfortunately many groups have dug in, feeling strongly that they know what is best for the fishery and the fish, which puts them at odds with one another.

The bluefin, a migratory species, carries no passport and knows no boundaries. The tuna can be in Canadian waters one day and American bays the next. They are known to travel across the Atlantic and into the Mediterranean Sea, adding Europe into the equation. Whose fish is it anyway?

Then there are governmental agencies. We have the U.S. National Marine Fisheries Service. Canada has an agency called Fisheries and Ocean Canada. The International Commission for Conservation of Atlantic Tunas (ICCAT) is responsible for the conservation of the species in the Atlantic Ocean.

I believe all of these groups and organizations have the best interest of the tuna fish front and center. I am a IGFA Certified Captain. As a harpooner, I'm also a member of the ABTA. I know first hand the passion each group brings to the table, and the pros and cons of the debate between them. I have sympathy for and understanding of the views on both sides. I would like nothing more than peace among all who chase the fish.

The bottom line is that the future of the bluefin fishery is in the hands of many people. The good news is that tuna stocks are as healthy as they have ever been in forty years. The schools of bluefin are growing. With so many people caring about these amazing fish, we can work together so that generations will continue to enjoy them without endangering them.

I understand there are groups, like Greenpeace, that want to protect the bluefin from me. It is true that I hunt the fish, I harvest them, and I get paid for killing them. I also love them. What Greenpeace should understand is that I and my brother tuna fishermen, be they hookers or harpooners, will never deplete the biomass. We care as much or more about the fish than all other parties because we live with them.

I came back into this fishery late in life for many reasons, and writing this book is a big part of it. I want my niece in California to read this story and be able to tell her friends what her Uncle Corky does for a living. I want people to remember Sonny McIntire, and I want people to know that commercial fishing is a livelihood worth defending. After all, we feed people.

Maggie's harpoon line coiled up in basket attached to harpoon ready to strike.
Photo from Decker

USGC boarding *Maggie* in 2017 and measuring legality of fish. Photo from Decker

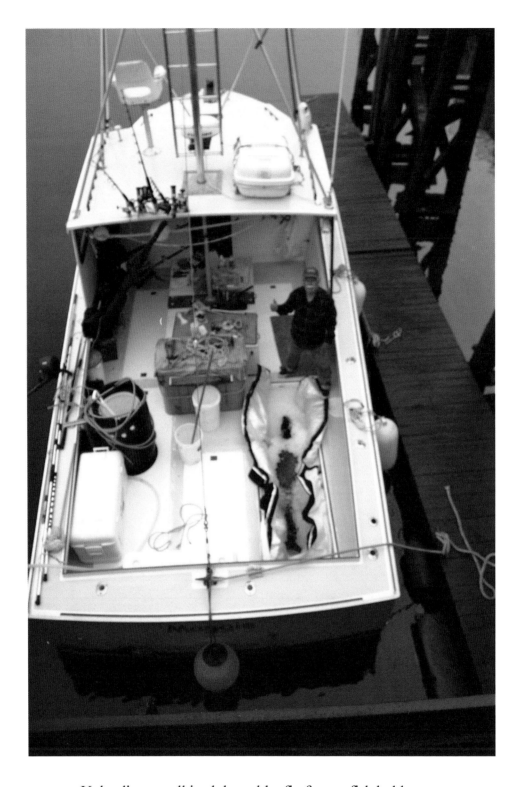

Unloading a well iced down bluefin from a fish hold on
Maggie with Mate Ricky Thurlow
Photo from Decker

21.

Swords

When I'm on a harpoon boat and I see a swordfish, I feel like I have been handed a gift from Neptune, the god of the sea. I've heard fishermen talk about swordfish everywhere from Kodiak, Alaska to Vanuatu in the South Pacific. The swordfish to a New England harpooner is the holy grail, the ultimate prize. They are the gladiators of the sea. The sight of a swordfish's dorsal fin and sickle-like tail is extremely rare. I've only seen five in my lifetime. Sonny McIntire says he's only seen one.

Swords are now part of the harpoon fishery. It is now legal to harpoon swordfish and sell them to a licensed dealer, which wasn't true just a few years ago. But even when we couldn't sell them, I've never heard of a harpooner who passed up the chance to iron them. Swordfish makes for great eating.

And they are easy to hunt. The swordfish only fears the mako shark, which will come in real fast and bite a sword in the tail to disable it. So as long as you do not approach a sword right on the tail, fishermen will tell you the fish will let you get close. They swim on the surface providing the proverbial barn door target. So the stories I hear of guys missing a sword are heart wrenching. I know from first-hand experience.

On July 6, 2016, Bradley and I had the first good harpoon day of the month. We heard a report of a body of tuna fish to the south in Murray Basin. But with only one good weather day, we decide to stay closer to home. We put in a full day in the shipping lanes off Portland. We saw a nice bunch of crashing fish on the Kettle on the way out. Birds were flying everywhere and occasionally whales and sunfish came to the surface.

Bradley and I looked at each other and said we need to stay right here. We worked the deep water in a slow lazy circle in a body of water called the Mistaken Grounds. The water conditions were the best a harpooner could wish for and we saw zero fish. There was a clear current line where the colder inshore dark green water was divided by a strong temperature break with the warmer dark deep blue water on the side. The difference was not small. The green water was sixty-one degrees; the blue water was sixty-nine degrees. After the one o'clock slack water tide change we still did not see even a flip from a bluefin.

We decided to head back inshore where we saw all the birds on the Kettle. Neither one of us could believe that the bluefin were not out in this beautiful warm blue water. At two o'clock, we returned to the green water. The birds were sitting on the water in large flocks. A few whales were lazily swimming about with full stomachs. The fish were on a major siesta. We didn't want to waste too much time there so we turned back offshore when Bradley pointed off the port bow.

"What is that, a bird?" As soon as I looked at where he was pointing, a fin, and the tail broke to full height.

"Sword!" I yelled. In a heartbeat, I ran out to the pulpit.

I could see the black shape of the fish about hundred and fifty feet away. It was a massive, a full grown female, in the five hundred pound class. It was basking in the sun, in the cold green water.

I remember thinking, "Why the hell is she in the green water?"
And then I thought, "Just hit it."

The *Maggie* is a fast boat, going six and a half knots, and I could see this gladiator more clearly as we came up on it. The swordfish was thick from head to tail, round and heavy. The broad bill that gives the fish its name was full foot across at the base of the head. The long bill tapered off to a fine point almost five feet in front of its huge saucer eyes. I pulled my arm back, holding the harpoon cocked over my right shoulder.

The swordfish was swimming erratically, as if it was confused about where it wanted to be. First, it was pointing away from us, then it turned sideways to the right. Bradley, knowing to approach from the side, slid me right up to that fish. I had it laid right out in front of me, and I just threw the pole right over its back. The harpoon skidded off the side of the fish.

How do you describe the feeling at that very moment in time? It's easy if you have ever missed an open net with a hockey puck in an overtime game, or taken your eyes off the road to look at your girlfriend and crashed your father's car. A gut wrenching, "Oh no, please, Can I just have a do-over? Can we rewind the tape?" It was one of those crushing moments we all have at some point in life.

Adding the fact that the fish was worth probably four or five thousand dollars and we hadn't caught a fish in over two weeks, my miss was a torture of both mind and spirit. I just missed.

That night I got a hold of an old buddy, Glenn Perkins, who I know from Perkins Cove. I wore my heart on my sleeve, told him about the horror show of missing that beast of a sword. He listened and then told me to get over it. Every fisherman has a story about a passenger named "Mr. Murphy,"the guy who brings with him Murphy's Law: "If anything can wrong, it will." Glenn told me about the time Mr. Murphy was on his boat.

"We arrive south of Murray's [Basin, located 40 miles off of Gloucester] and we find our first bunch, a herd, plowing along a bit deep I hit the fish back in the tail area and the zapper, numbs it. I walked the fish back to the stern and Mike puts a tail strap on the fish, we cleat it off, and the fish comes alive I thought it was going to tear the cleats out In about thirty seconds, the fish busts off everything and is gone."

"Holy shit,"I said, "That is crazy."

"I'm not done," he says. "About half an hour later we see the same fish towing about ten feet of line with it, and another big bunch pops up. I hit a monster, the shocker does not work and we put a flag out. We chased another couple of bunches and come back to the flag about an hour later. The fish is dead. We start hauling the hundred and fifty fathoms of line back and we are almost to the throwing line when we pull the dart- and lose the second one."

The moral to Glenn's story is, no matter how bad a day you are having, somebody somewhere is having a worse one. Everybody gets a visit from Mr. Murphy.

I had to find the courage to tell Sonny McIntire that I missed a swordfish as large as a bull moose. It took me two days. It was kind of like Luke Skywalker walking up to Yoda, and telling the master that the Dark Side was messing with him, and "Was it true that you could go deaf if you…" well, you get the picture.

I told Sonny about missing the swordfish and he stopped me halfway through.

"Did you throw over his back?" he asked.

I told him I did. The pole raked right down the fish's back. I overthrew the fish laid-out side too.

"I love your boat for going up on running tuna fish," he said. "It just pounces on the fish, but with what you are describing to me is, you went on that fish too fast. At that speed [6.5 knots] you wanted to take her head on or at the tail. Side, too. You should have kicked out of gear and just slid up to the fish."

"All right," I said hopefully "It's all Bradley's fault."

"No," Sonny told me. "You still missed a stupid easy shot, but that is why you missed."

Lesson learned. After speaking with the master, with a lifetime of experience, I knew exactly why I missed.

As soon as it happened, I tried to put my swordfish story down on paper and maybe get a little closure. I'm a proud person, and I love my fishery more than anything else in the world…my fishery. To be able to pursue this challenging lifestyle, I need to be successful. You are not successful missing swordfish. That just cannot happen. It'll be a long time before I'm over that day, and maybe I never really will be, but I can tell you this: I cannot wait to pick up that harpoon again.

Swordfish. Photo from Decker.

22.

Whales

When I was in my teens, we went out to meet the humpback whales of Stellwagen Bank because that's where the bluefin were likely to swim. The whale watching boats with sightseers from Cape Cod, Boston, and Gloucester were always hovering nearby. Captain Ahab had been succeeded by the tour boat skipper whose shipmates wielded cameras, not harpoons.

We were so close I could hear people dog cussing me for hunting whales. I would laugh while the ship's captains and crew calmed them down. The daily announcement on the loudspeaker of the boats informed their passengers that we, the harpooners, were not harming the whales. We were just chasing bluefin tuna.

Along with the finback, and minki whales, the humpbacks are an "indicator species".They indicate where the fish are. The humpbacks feed on sand eels that come into Massachusetts Bay in massive schools each summer. The poor eels, born in the middle of the Atlantic, are one to two inches long as they make their way toward the waters somewhere between Florida and Maine that they call home. The whales follow. They will "ball up" the eels by diving deep and blowing bubbles all around the outside of the eels, which makes it easy for the huge beast to feast on them. And the stripers, the seabirds, and the bluefin gather around to feast too. As harpooners, we know. We catch a lot of bluefin every year under the eyes of the whale watchers.

Tired of being observed, one harpooner took his revenge. His name was Gary Gerndy. In the 1980s, he fished with Bucko and he was-and is-one crazy Mainer. Back then Gary had long, long hair, but he was bald on top. He had a big bushy beard and was built like a linebacker. He told us he had a plan for entertaining the whale watchers. The next day, Bucko and Gary found themselves surrounded by four or five whale-watching boats. Eric Brazier and I were fishing about a hundred yards away.

Gary went up in the tower. He handed Bucko his glasses and hat. He shook out the huge mane of hair. He ripped off his shirt and he did a swan dive off the tower right into the middle of the feeding whales. When Gary broke the surface he was brandishing a huge Bowie knife in his right hand and screaming at the top of his lungs.

"Surrender your virgins and we will spare your lives," he yelled at the sea-going tourists.

Gary put the knife between his teeth and he starts swimming towards the nearest boat. Everyone of the whale watchers rushed to the opposite side of the boat, causing the ship to list hard the other way. I never laughed so hard in my whole life. The rest of the summer Gary and Bucko had the whales to themselves and the whale watchers gave their boat a wide berth.

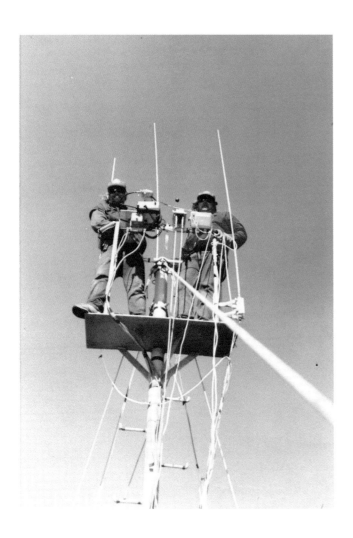

1980, Bucko and Gary on Bucko's boat, the *Jose B*. Photo from Burke Family

In the summer 2016, the humpbacks formed one massive herd. I have never seen so many whales gathered together. In June hundreds of humpbacks showed up on the backside of Cape Cod feeding on sand eels. Typically, the whales wait for the eels to come close to the shore but this year the whales ranged far offshore and intercepted the eels before they came into shallow water.

It was windy summer. As harpooners we need nice calm weather to be able to operate, and we could hardly string together two or three good days in a row all season. Each day we would have relocate the whales, because the bluefin never left those whales all summer long.

In early June, I was trying to locate the whales one morning around Wildcat Bank. We spent the night offshore hoping to be the first boat to find the massive body of humpies. A herd of whales that big is pretty easy to spot from the tower if you can just get in the right area where they happen to be feeding at daybreak. At seven in the morning I saw one boat steaming from the south; it was Sean Sullivan. I just turned our boat and followed him. He was heading farther offshore into Murray Basin. Twenty minutes later I started seeing the blowing of the whales.

Sean rode right into the middle of the largest concentration of whales and kicked his boat out of gear. I follow suit a couple hundred yards away. Pretty soon I heard an airplane and Norman showed up flying over his boat. I just watched them to see what the best tuna harpooning team in the world was going to do. Within a minute Sean was out in the stand, harpoon in hand. It wasn't long before he ironed a fish and put out a flag end, which told me he wasn't using his shocker.

My mate, Ricky Thurlow, and I just stared at how quick he was. We eased our boat right into the middle of the mayhem of bubble feeding whales. The humpbacks would break the surface all around the boat with huge gaping mouths. Out in the stand, harpoon in hand, I felt like I was in an IMAX theater: the overwhelming noise of the feeding whales, the powerful smell of the whales, the incredible sight of them soaring into the air, huge mouths opens, and then plunging back in the water. It took my breath away.

I had to remind myself why I was there and it wasn't for a National Geographic experience. In the turbulence of beasts and bubbles, the bluefin appeared, as if by magic. They came nose to nose with the humpbacks, gorging themselves on the tight balls of eels. I pulled the pole back and cocked my arms to throw. I picked out a big massive ball of eels and waited for a bluefin to appear in that spot.

Instead, a massive whale surfaced, with a mouth big enough to swallow a pickup truck, and devoured a mass of eels just fifteen feet in front of me. The giant head of that big bull rose up twenty feet in the air and I stared at his massive eyeball as he slid slowly back in the water. My heart stopped with the awe.

" To my right!" Ricky yelled, shaking me out of my whale trance. Six bluefin in the five hundred pound range were floating in the water twenty feet away. They were just hanging out, lined up and waiting their turn for the eel. I threw at the nearest fish and missed high. The fish were quite a bit deeper than they appeared. I pulled the pole back. There were still four more right there. I didn't miss the second time and we hit the shocker.

The whales, the sand eels, and the tuna felt the electric jolt in the water, and it just seemed to piss off all of them, except for the fish I just hit, because he was dead. Lesson learned again. If the best harpooner in the world isn't zapping the fish with the shocker, he probably has a good reason for it. We educate the tuna in a group every single time we zap one of the school. They know who we are.

And so it went all summer. That body of whales would be on Platts one day, sixty nautical miles away on Wildcat the next. They would be loafing in two hundred feet of water off Chatham, Mass. Or swimming eight hundred foot deep Murray's Basin. We never knew where they would be found until the next good day we had. On the radio, my buddy Greg Gibbs wouldn't even ask me if I saw any running fish. His only question was, "You with the whales?" Greg knew that everything else would fall into place if we stayed close to the whales.

I have always known the bluefin are exceptionally intelligent. That summer I also learned they can be bullies. The pilots noticed it first. On the radio I heard Mark Brochu telling Jackie Cadario that he was seeing bluefin following blue sharks, commonly known as "blue dogs." He was saying he saw four fish harassing a blue dog.

I did not believe it until I saw it with my own eyes. We had spotted a blue dog fin and tails, and then we saw a pair of tuna fish, swimming on either side. One fish would grab a hold of the shark's long pectoral fin and hold on. The shark would try and pull away. The fish would release the shark, and the bluefin on the other side would suckle onto the other fin and give the shark a good shake. They were bullying the blue dog. I threw my harpoon at one of those big bastards, and I missed because I was laughing so hard.

The bluefin bullies were the talk of Gloucester. Jackie said he and Mark saw tuna harassing a blue dog five times that day and he saw it three more times on his own. Jackie did not think tuna beating up on blue dogs was as funny as I did, and so he kept his wits about him. He managed to harpoon a couple of fish while they were busy playing with the blue dogs.

By late July the tuna fish were massing in huge bunches, a pretty good sign that they would soon move on as a group. But the fish would not part from the large body of humpbacks. In a single afternoon, I saw what I guess was more than five thousand bluefin in the vicinity of the whales.

Ricky and I chased over twenty bunches that day. Some of these bunches had up to five hundred fish in the herd. And finally we got one! But the fish were so wild that a lot of guys did not get any that day. Everybody was in the stand for hours and no one was doing any real business. So it went through the summer of 2016. If we only had the good weather days, I think it would have been an epic season. Instead it was a bummer of a summer for everyone, except the whales.

Happy minki whale. Photo from Decker.

Humpback whales frolicking. Photo from Decker

Aerial of humpback whale

Photo from Brochu

23.

Full Circle

In the summer 2015, Bradley's son, Jeremy was entering his senior year in high school. As a holder of a student lobster license, he needed to log sea time. So when Bradley took him out to haul lobsters, I would take people along to do some harpooning. Introducing people to my world and writing about it may not be profitable but it makes for good times and great memories. I can see why Carl McIntire took us kids along all those years ago.

In early July, I had a couple of friends up from Florida, Ed and his wife Amy, so I took them with me. On the ride out, I gave Ed a five-minute rundown on the basics of harpooning on the ride out: *"you're going to drive the boat. When I see a tuna fish you want to try to run right over it with the boat. I'll tell you where to go. Just follow my pole."*

We ran into the fish right away, in the shipping lanes off Portland, a couple of hours out of Boothbay. Ed got to practice on a running bunch of fish. The fish did not stay up in the water, so they were hard to track. But Ed quickly gained some understanding of the game. Within an hour we spotted a couple more bunches and then a pair plowing the water. These two fish were so far apart they were almost like two singles. Yet they were swimming together. They must have been husband and wife.

Ed, in the tower, was "seeing color" on his very first bluefin. He was not sure which one to follow. I was pointing my pole at the fish on the left fish, but he ignored me and he split the distance between the two. I throw out and slightly behind at the fish on the left who was about a boat length away. The pole went under the fish's belly. If Ed had followed the pole and lined up one or the other, the fish would have been under my feet, an easy shot, what we call a "barn door," a can't-miss opportunity.

` But we missed it.

Later that month, I gave two Boothbay high school boys, Devyn and Jacob, their first ever harpoon experience. As we headed out I remembered how little training I had given Ed, so I really worked Devyn and Jacob like we were at football practice. We practiced by approaching lobster buoys, throwing the pole, taking the boat out of gear, and most important, following the pole. This is absolutely key: *follow the pole.*

After an hour of practice, we decided that Devyn would drive the boat. It was a really nice day, a light wind from the southwest, streaking a calm surface. Twenty miles offshore, we find a single, a huge fish swimming erratically. I looked both boys in the eyes: 'Follow my pole." I headed for the pulpit, full of confidence. This fish was going on ice!

The fish had other ideas. He would swim south and then veer off due east for a hundred yards. Then he would decide north was a good direction. I think he might have been mentally slow for a tuna, but he was a monster. The *Maggie* does six and a half knots in gear, so we lined him up quite fast. In ten strokes of his tail, he made a ninety degree turn. I pointed at the fish, now only three boat lengths out. I could see the whole fish, all eight hundred pounds of him. We make up the three boat lengths in a couple of heartbeats. It was so exciting the boys followed the tuna fish with their eyes and forgot about steering. I watched helplessly as the fish went one way and we went the other. That giant was never seen again.

I was boiling mad at Devyn and Jacob. That fish was the big one I had been waiting all year for, and they had let him get way. I bit my tongue, shut my mouth, restrained myself. I could remember making that kind of a mistake at their age. Seeing a running bluefin for the first time can really mess with your head. Plus, that was the day I messed up the wiring on the shocker, so we didn't have an electric harpoon.

Patiently, I went over what they needed to do if we were going to have any chance of catching a fish. Both boys were still talking when I looked up to see a triple a couple hundred yards off. I looked Devyn in the eyes, and told him to stay calm.

"Just follow the pole," I said.

I ran back out into the stand. These three fish were running about ten feet apart. They were in the four hundred pound range, showing a decent wake, and most importantly, running in a nice straight line.

Devyn rode me right up to the middle fish, like he had been doing this every day of his life. I waited until the fish were about fifteen feet out and then I threw at the back of the middle fish. The harpoon hit an inch to the right of its dorsal fin, and the fish reacted with a whitewater explosion. The throwing line ripped out of the bucket as the fish blasted off towards the bottom.

This fish was really going. It was time for Jacob to untie the flag end and he didn't do anything. I made it to the roof in time to grab the flag end and throw it overboard. The flag hit the water and immediately was pulled under by the racing bluefin.

I looked up to Jacob and asked him why he didn't untie the flags.

"I never seen anything," he kept saying over and over, while Devyn was still in the tower chanting "Holy shit! Holy shit!"

I told the two boys we need to locate that flag as soon as possible. Without the flags untied, we might have problem recovering the fish.

We started marking up the map on the flat screen computer in the house of the boat, keeping track of where we looked so we'd be able to find the fish once it died. I saw another harpoon boat and we asked the crew to keep an eye out for our flag, as we continued the search.

Two nervous hours later, we stumbled upon the flag three miles offshore from where we ironed the fish. The fish was dead. It wasn't large, dressing three hundred and sixty six pounds, but to these two young men, that was one big ass tuna fish. They earned their first tuna check. It will be interesting to see if this day will turn them into future harpooners.

Two new harpooners, maybe. Photo from Decker

On another Monday I invited my buddy Megan to come with me when I was taking the boat down to Perkins Cove. Megan is a cop in the town of Saco, where she drives the police force's patrol boat. She loves to fish and hunt, and she is one hell of a photographer.

Along the way, we saw a single that got away before we could act. An hour later, outside of the Jeffreys Bank, we spotted another single that was really moving. I pointed at the fish's wake about three hundred yards out.

"You got it?" I asked her

No, she said. She didn't see it. Still pointing, I turned the boat to get behind the running fish, yelling out distance and range. Still Megan could not see the fish, which was just two hundred yards out. I kicked the boat out of gear and pointed my arm right down Megan's nose at the fish. She still could not pick it up. I was about to freak out when the fish goes airborne,

"I got him!" Megan yelled.

The fish jumped two or three more times and then disappeared forever. Oh well. It was a beautiful day on the water and we learned an old lesson once again: It takes time to become a harpooner.

After Billy Mac passed in 2013, Sonny McIntire stopped tuna fishing. I could understand but for me this was so sad. Not seeing the McIntire boat on the water just wasn't right. I hounded Sonny and finally he agreed, maybe to just shut me up. I also talked his two sons, Bobby and Shane, into taking off a few days off from lobstering to go harpooning.

Finally, on July 22, 2015, we departed at seven thirty in the morning headed for Cape Cod. Weather wise, the day was not optimal for harpooning. In fact, it was rough as hell, but I did not care. I had the best harpooner who ever lived on my boat and we were going fishing.

We ran at fifteen knots, traveling seventy miles to the backside of Cape Cod, out to the deep water, beyond the shipping lanes. The sea was so rough we could only have two people in the tower, Shane and I; Sonny and Bobby rode the roof. When we arrived at a spot where we knew some fish had been caught recently, we found about a dozen harpoon boats and five or six planes working the area.

Sonny spotted the first bunch of the day--from the roof. Both Shane and I looked at each other in embarrassment. Even at seventy five Sonny could see fish better than us, and he didn't even have to be twenty five feet in the air to do it. I watched nervously as Sonny made his way out onto the pulpit, standing harpoon in hand above six-foot waves.

This bunch of fish was massive: three hundred or more fins and tails showing, as they milled about in a huge circle. Sonny took a hard shot at a deep fish. He missed.

 "Corky we just have to find another bunch," Shane said to me. "We cannot let the last fish he throws at be a miss."

 I never looked so hard in my whole life for a tuna fish as I did that day. I prayed to any God who would listen: Give us one more chance. I did not care if I saw another fish all summer. Please, I said silently. I must have said it a hundred times.

Then Shane spotted another bunch. Or maybe it was the same one. Shane took his time steering the boat around the bunch to get down wind on them. We got Sonny safely back out on the pulpit, and lined up on the fish. It was so rough Shane was steering the boat with one hand and holding onto me with the other as I took photos of Sonny.

This time he waited and though my camera lens I saw Sonny throw. Sonny numbed a fish right under his feet but the shocker did not work so we had to put out a flag end on the struck fish. I started praying again: *Please don't pull the dart. Please don't pull the dart.*

The fish pulled the flag under for about five minutes before popping back up and towing the flag offshore. We followed looking for other bunches. The fish stopped towing the flag. We grabbed a hold of the line and started to pull the fish to the boat. It was still alive but weak. We soon had it in the door. It wasn't a monster, under four hundred pounds, but it was the most beautiful bluefin I have ever seen.

We were seventy seven miles from Perkins Cove so we had a long rough steam in. We arrived back at the dock at twelve thirty that night, where we finally offloaded Sonny's fish. I was mentally and physically worn out, but I could not fall asleep for hours. I kept reliving that moment over and over I thought my head would split apart from the stupid grin on my face. My childhood hero, at seventy five years old, had harpooned a fish off my boat,

The next morning at eight a.m., I saw Sonny go by me in his boat heading out to haul his lobster gear. I'd been up all night. The old man had no trouble sleeping. I had come full circle in life.

Seventy five year old Sonny poised to throw. Photo from Decker

Bingo! Sonny, 2015. Photo from Decker

Sonny McIntire with sons, Shane and Bobby, 2015. Photo from Decker

24.

Hooking

For every boat chasing bluefin with a harpoon, there are five or more boats fishing for them with rod and reel. Every season far more fish are caught on a hook than a harpooner. The rod and reel guys, or the 'hookers' as they are known, have a much longer season to harvest fish. They can hook them in almost any weather, and they can fish from just about anything that floats from twenty-foot outboard skiffs to multi million-dollar sport fishing vessels. The harpoon boats general category allows a boat to catch fish by hook or harpoon, and the daily limit of four fish makes this category the preferred option for up to ninety five percent of the boats.

In August 2015 I joined them. I was in learning mode. I spent hundreds of hours, either drifting or anchored up, with live baits in the water. I got exactly one bite; we even managed to boat the beast. But for the amount of time and effort we put in, it was a massive disappointment. Hooking bluefin commercially is not an easy trade. The high-liners (best fishermen)   know the small tricks in the trade and their boats are customized for rod and reeling. By contrast, we did not know the tricks and the *Maggie i*s a far cry from a rod and reel rig.

The one fish we caught came on September 18th on Georges Bank. When we arrived on the Bank on the 17th, we were still rigged up for harpooning and looking for late season tuna and swordfish. We found a fleet of rod and reel boats. We joined in, using what we had on hand, frozen ballyhoo, as bait. We managed to jig up some live mackerel too but the time we got our act together the fishing was pretty much over.

The following morning we joined the fleet in hooking. At nine am one of our reels went off. Fish on the line! Bradley has a lot more experience rod and reeling tuna than I do, so he manned the rod while I drove the boat. That crazed fish stayed near the surface as it ripped off tremendous blistering runs, tearing hundreds of yards of line. After an hour the fish tired enough that we managed to see it for the first time. It was not huge but good-sized: around four hundred and fifty pounds,

I threw a harpoon and missed. The fish wanted nothing to do with the boat and managed to sound straight down to the bottom. The second time we got the fish close enough to the boat, I got a dart in it and that was it, game over. We tail wrapped the fish and lifted it onto the boat and then we sat on the rail exhausted from the excitement. We would spend the rest of the day drifting with the fleet, hoping for another bite, but that was it for us. With bad weather coming we made the one hundred and fifty mile ride back to Boothbay.

I have a new respect for this fishery. Being a harpooner I never really paid a lot of attention to the hookers. None of the rod and reel boats was in our network, so I never knew much about them. The equipment is expensive. Custom tuna rods can cost more than a thousand dollars. The one hundred and thirty pound test class reels go for twelve hundred to fifteen hundred dollars each. The hook boats also have live bait tanks, banks of sodium lights that turn night into day, top of the line electronics, and generators. The list goes on and on.

The *Maggie* is not equipped with any of this. I have about ten thousand dollars invested in my rods and reels but that is pretty much the extent of my equipment. It will take a huge investment for me to rig up properly for this fishery in the future.

In the North Atlantic, the fall comes on fast. The summer blue warmth of the August sun turns quickly into the bitter cold of a September nor'easter. My Florida buddy Gary Carter was returning from his yearly trip to Canada where he failed to catch a bluefin for the first time. He arrived from Antigonish with tales of bad weather and losing fish. On the last day he was there, the body of fish moved completely on his last day. He had spent ten grand for zero fish. Now he was coming with me. If we caught one on the rod and reel, we'd get paid, or so we hoped.

Bradley was more than happy to wish us luck as he returned to his business on land, tending the moorings in Boothbay, and preparing for his winter boat project. Gary and I quickly figured that the *Maggie* needed upgrades before she was seaworthy. The two of us, green as the grass in the hooking game, put in a huge effort. The results were less than huge.

It's not like we didn't see bluefin. They were feeding all around us and we had baits in the water. They just weren't biting. The weather turned so cold that the condensation from our breathing would freeze above our bunks into icicles. Our only heat was a two-burner gas cooking stove. Our bathroom was a gallon bucket. We were bobbing in five-foot seas and it was raining. You get the picture.

We did have one bite in those torture-filled days-sort of. Gary, being the best ground fisherman I have ever met, was fishing for live bait all the time, so we were well-stocked. One morning, he caught a huge squid. We were anchored up just south of Portland about ten miles offshore. I was just about to put out a line with live mackerel, so I quickly changed my bait to that two-foot long squid. I put a live bait hook though the upper mantle in the squid. The creature took off in a blast of ink when I placed the hook in the water. I set the balloon at sixty feet, meaning the squid was swimming on the hook 60 feet below the water's surface.

That thing wasn't in the water five minutes when we started marking tuna fish under the boat. They were feeding. The rod loaded up like we had a bite-and then went slack. Not a single click of drag was taken. I pulled the bait back to see what happened.

The head of the squid was gone, and the body looked like it had been held to a belt sander. A bluefin had bit its damn head off. The hook never even got in the fish's mouth. Bad luck? Or had I made a rookie mistake? All I know for sure is that tuna fish love squid.

And that was our only bite. When Gary and I lost our anchor in thirty knots of north wind, we called it quits. We steamed the *Maggie* back to Boothbay for the last time in 2015. We are snowbirds. We live in Florida for a reason. It was time to migrate south.

Gary Carter hooked up
and with the catch on
Maggie 2016. Photos from
Decker

Gary with whopping 98 inch bluefin, Jeffreys, August
2017 Photo from Decker

25.

Gene Pool of the Gods

A bluefin tuna can live for thirty, forty or fifty years or more. The oldest fish can reach incredible size. The Small Point Fish in the youth of Merle Gilliam and Carl McIntire are probably all gone today, but the offspring of these fish, I do believe, are the giants of Antigonish today. I am a fisherman, not a scientist, so I don't know how to prove they are same fish, but I know in my gut that they are.

I continue on my quest to know their secrets. Where do they come from before they arrive in northern Nova Scotia every summer? Where do they go when they leave the bay? Maybe the tagging program started in 2015 will shed some light on the gene pool of the gods. Until then I can only theorize and speculate.

I have to believe that a creature as smart as a giant bluefin will find a way to keep its bloodline going generation after generation. I know that the Small Point Fish have, over the span of my lifetime, found ways to avoid pursuit. They know to avoid the harpoon boats and the seiners. They know where they can safely travel. They know where the herring are, and where they can spawn without danger.

Am I giving a fish too much credit? I don't think so. I have spent too many hours in pursuit of them to underestimate them. I think my observations give them the respect that they have earned.

My trip to Canada in 2014 changed my life. I saw first hand what I have spent almost fifty years dreaming about. I am once again deeply involved in world of the bluefin, and I'll spend the rest of my days on this earth in quest of these grand fish.

People ask me how can I kill something I love so much. I'm a fisherman. It is all I have ever known. I know the Small Point Fish are alive today. They have found a safe haven in the northern waters of Canada. If I lived up north I am sure I would be a charter boat captain escorting catch-and-release fishermen to the feeding grounds. The hand of fate made me a Maine harpooner, so that is what I do. I will never reach the level of Sonny McIntire, hell no. What I will do is follow in his footsteps. With the time remaining to me, I'm going to write about and share what I know about the wonders of the bluefin tuna.

In late May 2016 I was sitting on my boat in Boothbay Harbor two days before the harpoon season was to begin. It was damp, cold and pouring rain. I had a lot of things to do but instead I was reflecting.

The day before I drove to Perkins Cove to meet Jackie Cadario and Glenn Perkins to get three VHF radios. Glenn is from the family that gave Perkins Cove its name. Jackie is the son of the late Jack Cadario, the man who let me throw for the first time.

I last saw Jackie in 1984 when I fished one last Maine summer before moving to Alaska. It's been more than thirty years since I've seen my friend. He still looked like I remembered him but he talked like his father, even walked like him.

We talked with Sonny, Shane and Bobby McIntire on their boat *Queen of Peace,* which was getting a new diesel engine installed. We helped fetch Glenn's mast and pulpit. We drove a flatbed truck with a pulpit strapped to the top looking like something out of a Mad Max movie, through the crowds of tourists swarming Perkins Cove on Memorial Day weekend. It was like stepping back in time.

At one time we had eight people man handling Glenn's twenty foot-long pulpit down a gangway over a series of floating docks, to hang it off the bow of his boat. I looked up to see about a hundred tourists watching us and taking photos. Much has changed but Perkins Cove is still the center of the harpooners' world. We, the harpooners are few, and the many tourists were fascinated by what we do.

After we put Glenn's stand on, I said my goodbyes to everyone and made my way up to the office of Fred Mayo, Ogunquit's Harbor Master. Fred is one of my favorite people in the whole world, a generation older than I am, When I was growing up, he was one of the young tuna/ lobstermen with his first boat. He took me out on his lobster boat to haul the tub trawls they set out every spring. He and his mate Cory Staples knew I loved the anticipation of seeing those baited hooks come back, hopefully with a halibut, but usually a whale codfish. They always had room for a skinny ten year old kid who wanted to fish.

I had to get up to Sonny's house and see his wife Alicia before picking up some aluminum pipe I had stored at a friend's house. I reluctantly cut our time short. Fred told me he had a mooring for me, and hoped I'd bring the boat down to the cove.

At Alicia's, she had just come back from church. We sat in their sun room, looking over a few old family albums and remembering the old days. She gave me some photos. I kissed her goodbye, and braved the traffic on Route One all the way back to Boothbay.

As I drank my coffee, waiting for the rain to stop I thought, I'll be fifty four years old this summer? How the hell did it all happen so quickly?

I thought how lucky I am to be in good enough health, both in mind and body, to enjoy camping out on a harpoon boat at this stage of my life. I'm married to the perfect woman who tries so hard to be supportive. I thought: there is nowhere else I'd rather be,

In 48 hours I would be looking for the first bluefin bunch of the year. I'm living the dreams of that five-year-old boy who looked his father in the eye, as he wrapped his son in a towel trying to keep the tuna blood and slime from getting all over the backseat of his car.

"Dad," I said. "I'm going be a harpooner when I grow up."

I called that one right.

Corky and Sonny McIntire, Perkins Cove, July 2015. Photo from Tibbets

Maggie. Aerial photo from Davies

26.

Wicked Tuna

The epicenter of New England tuna fishing is now Gloucester Massachusetts. But Gloucester is not a commercial fishing port as it was in my youth. The vast ground-fish fleet has been replaced by a handful of large mid-water trawlers. Only a fraction of the dragger-boats that fish by dragging nets-that docked there from the 1960's to the 1980's still remain. The diverse commercial fleet from days of yore now consists of a fleet of tuna boats, made up of a small squadron of harpoon boats to a massive fleet of rod reel boats.

Gloucester is so busy these days that I have a hard time finding a good place to keep the *Maggie*, which has a thirty-foot pulpit standing over the bow. Last summer I simply rafted the *Maggie*, in other words tied it to the *Coot*, Dana Kangas's boat. Their was just no dock space available. Many harpoon boats have to lift their pulpits up to fit in a slip. While I can lift my pulpit into the air, and swing it aft to lay against my tower, it is a daunting task and not one I would want to undertake every night, so we usually raft up in Gloucester.

One reason why the Gloucester harbor is so crowded these days is 'Wicked Tuna', National Geographic's hour long, weekly reality television show, with a whole lot of re-runs thrown in. Now in its sixth season 'Wicked Tuna' only depicts fishermen engaged in rod and reeling bluefin tuna off the New England coast (a southern version called 'Outer Banks' is coming soon). "Wicked Tuna" has certainly benefited Gloucester, bringing attention to local businesses and well known fishermen. Many stores now sell the 'Wicked Tuna' clothing line.

When I first heard about 'Wicked Tuna' a few years ago, I was excited. I thought a program about our fishery would not only be a cool TV experience that would introduce people to my harpoon passion. But, 'Wicked Tuna' didn't get around to including harpooners until season five in 2015 when episode's four and six, followed two harpoon boats, the *Lily* captained by Bill Muniz and guided by his pilot Mark Brochu, and the *Kristiana,* captained by Greg Chorebanian and assisted by harpooner Greg Gibbs.

The first show I saw depicted some of the guys having a punch up on a dock, something I have never witnessed or heard of. The treatment of harpooning bore no resemblance to the world I know, and I stopped watching it. I just hit the clicker and went back to the NFL Network, disgusted with the thought that the general public would come away with the impression we are a bunch of thugs beating the crap out of each other.

This is not a knock on the guys who participated in the show. Bill Muniz and the two Gregs are some of the most talented harpooners on the water. The only hooker on the show whom I know somewhat personally is Tyler McLaughlin (also the guy that was getting beat up on the show). Tyler is a young fisherman from New Hampshire, who is probably one of the top three hook fishermen in the world when it comes to bluefin. He appears in every show and is one of the series main characters.

In 2016 the harpoon boats were written out of the show, and I only heard rumors about the reasoning behind the decision. I asked Mark Brochu why and he told me he was never given a reason, except that the decision originated with National Geographic, which apparently decided harpooning did not fit the theme of the show. Mark said he also received the message, "don't go away," so perhaps 'Wicked Tuna' will return to the harpooners someday. I hope so.

I suspect that harpooning may be a little too much like hunting for those who want to sell a fishing show. Last summer, one sportfishing magazine editor who I often work for, told me he wanted a couple of pieces, "before you go off to murder bluefin." It struck me a lot of my peers from the sportfishing world may view harpooning like he does-as barbaric or cruel-and that might explain why 'Wicked Tuna' ignores harpoon boats. The truth is nobody knows except the people at National Geographic.

I can understand why someone who knows zero about our fishery might have a slanted view if all they know is that we electrocute tuna fish. But this is an over-simplification of our fishery. In fact, it takes a lot more talent to harpoon a bluefin tuna than it does to catch one on a hook. And it is less painful to the fish. A tuna that bites on a hook spends it last moments fighting for its life, sometimes for hours. The fish is then brought to the boat exhausted and has its gills slashed, and bled out alongside the vessel. In contrast, a fish harvested by harpoon dies instantly; it does not suffer.

In addition, harpooning is the only fishery that has zero by-catch, meaning the inadvertent catching of fish of other species. When hooking, if you put a live bait in the water, and any fish that can fit that bait in its mouth is going to try and eat it, including sharks. I have caught so many blue sharks while hooking for tuna that sometimes I have had to just pull my anchor and move on. I spent a large portion of my life in the Bering Sea operating factory trawlers in the ground-fish industry where the by-catch was generally huge and damaging, so I'm a bloody expert on the subject of by-catch!

In contrast, harpooners only throw at swordfish or bluefin tuna. That's why the Whole Foods grocery chain refuses to sell swordfish caught on long-liners. They only sell 'harpoon caught swordfish'. They know we are careful! I am no expert on the show, I'd have to actually watch it to have an opinion. So to me, 'Wicked Tuna', may be great for Gloucester; not so great for harpooning, the purest commercial fishery on today's greener planet.

Gaint bluefin on ice.
Photo from Robichaud

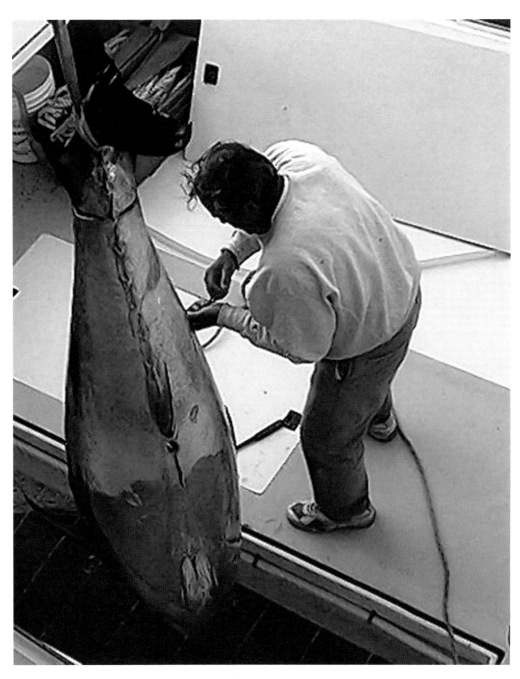

David Linney with harpooned bluefin.
Photo from Robichaud

Epilogue

The Small Point Fish are now generations removed from their namesake. Once again they number in the hundreds of thousands. The school's younger generation has grown to breeding size in fewer years than the ones before. The rich herring in the safe waters of Canada are more plentiful and easier to catch every feeding season. The northern feeding grounds are now a safe haven for the fish. The small boats even feed them.

The new spawning grounds, in the deep water of the mid-Atlantic, have been a kept secret for generations. The real old fish still remember the hunted days. They still steer the school clear of the killing grounds. In the fall, the fish leave the bay once again, all within a few days of each other. The cold water triggers the move.

After one last massive feed day, eating more than enough, the fish turn towards deeper water. They are content. Their fat stores will sustain them on the migration and through the breeding season just ahead. They turn tail on the herring and the men on the boats wave them on. Until next summer, when the fish will arrive, lean and hungry, their beautiful bay awaits the return of the great school.

The Small
Point Fish

Photo from
Brochu

134

And still we hunt them…

Harpooner David Linney after running bunch. Photo from Robichaud

83553449R00082

Made in the USA
Columbia, SC
11 December 2017